THE

ETHNIC AND GROUP IDENTITY MOVEMENTS

EARNING RECOGNITION

The Abolitionist Movement

The Civil Rights Movement

The Environmental Movement

The Ethnic and Group Identity Movements

The Family Values Movement

The Labor Movement

The Progressive Movement

The Women's Rights Movement

REFORM MOVEMENTS
IN AMERICAN
HISTORY

THE

ETHNIC AND GROUP IDENTITY MOVEMENTS

EARNING RECOGNITION

Ann Malaspina

Series Editor
Tim McNeese

CHELSEA HOUSE
PUBLISHERS

An imprint of Infobase Publishing

To my parents, Alex and Doris Malaspina, who have made the
world a better place through hard work and benevolence.

Cover: Left to right: same-sex marriage proponents, Native American rights supporters, and advocates of the disabled show their support for each cause.

The Ethnic and Group Identity Movements: Earning Recognition

Copyright © 2008 by Infobase Publishing

Chelsea House
An imprint of Infobase Publishing
132 West 31st Street
New York NY 10001

Library of Congress Cataloging-in-Publication Data
Malaspina, Ann, 1957-
 The Ethnic and group identity movements : earning recognition / Ann Malaspina.
   p. cm. -- (Reform movements in American history)
 Includes bibliographical references and index.
 ISBN-13: 978-0-7910-9571-3 (hardcover)
 ISBN-10: 0-7910-9571-1 (hardcover)
 1. Minorities--Civil rights--United States--Juvenile literature. 2. Civil rights move-
ments--United States--Juvenile literature. 3. Social movements--United States--
Juvenile literature. 4. United States--Ethnic relations--Juvenile literature. 5. United
States--Social conditions--1945---Juvenile literature. 6. Group identity--United States-
-Juvenile literature. 7. Pluralism (Social sciences)--United States--Juvenile literature. I.
Title. II. Series.
 E184.A1M264 2007
 323.173--dc22
                                      2007021721

Chelsea House books are available at special discounts when purchased in bulk
quantities for businesses, associations, institutions, or sales promotions. Please call our
Special Sales Department in New York at (212) 967-8800 or (800) 322-8755.

You can find Chelsea House on the World Wide Web at http://www.chelseahouse.com

Series design by Kerry Casey
Cover design by Ben Peterson
Printed in the United States of America
Bang EJB 10 9 8 7 6 5 4 3 2 1

This book is printed on acid-free paper.

All links and Web addresses were checked and verified to be correct at the time of publication. Because of the dynamic nature of the Web, some addresses and links may have
changed since publication and may no longer be valid.

CONTENTS

1

The Urge for Freedom

In April 1963, civil rights organizers launched a campaign to end segregation in Birmingham, Alabama, one of the largest industrial cities in the South. They sat at segregated lunch counters and boycotted downtown merchants. They marched on city hall and protested at the public library, which was segregated and closed to black patrons. Every day, the protests grew larger, and many people were arrested. On Good Friday, April 12, police arrested the civil rights leader, the Reverend Martin Luther King Jr. Dr. King used his time in jail to write a letter to a group of Alabama clergymen who had criticized the civil rights movement. "Oppressed people cannot remain oppressed forever. The urge for freedom will eventually come,"[1] Dr. King wrote in his now famous "Letter from Birmingham Jail." Soon after the Birmingham protests, President John F. Kennedy introduced civil rights legislation in Congress. The following year, Congress passed the landmark Civil Rights Act of 1964, opening the doors to opportunity and equal rights for African Americans.

Dr. King's "urge for freedom" inspired not just African Americans but many groups of people who lived at the margins of society. United by a particular characteristic, such as ethnic origin, race, age, or disability, identity groups emerged during the 1960s and began pushing for change. People who had felt isolated by their experiences joined with others like themselves. These groups of gays and lesbians, American Indians, Asian Americans, senior citizens, people with disabilities, and many others tried to make their voices heard. They pressed for respect, civil rights, freedoms, and a larger role in American society.

This era of social upheaval and political unrest in the United States energized the identity groups and paved the way for the critical reforms they were seeking. Popular folk musicians Bob Dylan and Joan Baez sang songs such as "Blowin' in the Wind" about the oppressed rising up. In Washington, D.C., political leaders took a new look at the disadvantaged and disenfranchised. In his State of the Union speech on January 8, 1964, President Lyndon Johnson announced the War on Poverty to lift up the "many Americans [who] live on the outskirts of hope." The government "must pursue poverty, pursue it wherever it exists—in city slums and small towns, in sharecropper shacks or in migrant worker camps, on Indian Reservations, among whites as well as Negroes, among the young as well as the aged, in the boom towns and in depressed areas,"[2] said Johnson.

"COMING OUT OF THE CLOSET"

For the many living "on the outskirts of hope," a spark had been lit, and a new period of progress began. People with disabilities pushed for access to public buses and buildings, and appropriate education programs in public schools. American Indians demanded the right to practice their native religions and fish on their traditional lands. Chicanos advocated for bilingual education so that their children could learn English and still keep up with classes in Spanish. People found they could achieve more as a group than they ever had as individuals. Many of their efforts were successful. They helped to change laws, build new support programs, and influence the political process.

Shortly after he took over as president when John F. Kennedy was assassinated in late 1963, Lyndon B. Johnson announced that he would introduce legislation to combat poverty in the United States. By the time Johnson took office, the national poverty rate stood at 19 percent. Johnson is pictured here with his wife, Lady Bird, visiting a home in the impoverished Appalachian region of Kentucky in April 1964.

Most of the groups used nonviolent tactics, but long-simmering anger sometimes led to violence and clashes with police, as when Chicanos in East Los Angeles took to the streets in August 1970.

The gay rights movement called it "coming out of the closet," and others were doing it, too. Rather than hide and be ashamed of their sexual identity, as they had been taught, gay men and lesbians marched through the streets of New York City and San Francisco waving rainbow flags in noisy and outrageous gay pride marches, starting in the late 1960s.

People in wheelchairs rolled through the streets of Seattle and Boston, daring anyone to deny them the same right as everyone else to board buses and go to school. American Indians who had for decades been forced to speak English in schools now held classes to learn their native languages. Even senior citizens sought to dispel negative views of old age; instead, celebrating their maturity and experience, while seeking pensions and healthcare benefits. For many people, the drive to gain pride in their identity was as important as convincing Congress to pass a new law.

CHANGE AND CONTROVERSY

These identity and reform movements transformed American society in fundamental ways, from new civil rights laws to more accepting attitudes toward diversity. By learning more about those groups whose experiences were so different from their own, people became more tolerant. Yet the push for reform by identity groups was often controversial. Giving special rights to certain people, or advocating one group's agenda over another's, creates the potential for sparking new divisions and inequalities.

Affirmative action is one example. Designed to redress the United States' history of racial and sexual discrimination, affirmative action grants advantages to minorities or women in order to give everyone the same opportunities. Proponents say affirmative action is necessary because certain groups are still disadvantaged by history, discrimination, and other circumstances. Critics say affirmative action gives unfair advantages and penalizes whites and men, and that people should be judged on their qualifications, not their racial or sexual identity. Some minorities feel that affirmative action gives a negative perception that they benefited from an unfair advantage and did not earn their position. Others disagree. They point out that, since minorities and women still earn less than white men and face discrimination in educational and career advancement, affirmative action has a place in certain circumstances.

Identity movements also raise questions about the nature of American society. Is it a multicultural melting pot or a collection of diverse communities, each with their own interests and agendas? After tensions between African Americans and Koreans in a Los Angeles neighborhood erupted in riots in 1992, some people questioned whether it was possible for them to live together. "We began to examine whether or not multiculturalism is a myth," says Edward Chang, a professor of ethnic studies at the University of California, Riverside. "The

During the 1992 Los Angeles riots, violence erupted between Korean Americans and African Americans after a Korean shop owner shot Latasha Harlins, a 15-year-old African American. Since the riots, both groups have worked together to improve their relationship. Jae Yul Kim, who had to rebuild after the riots, is pictured here greeting longtime customer McKinley Gipson at his market in South Central Los Angeles.

riots showed that perhaps white, black, Asian, and Hispanic are still all-too-separate, unequal societies."[3]

SAYING MY NAME

Gaining pride in one's identity changes personal lives as well as the public landscape. Increasingly, immigrants learned to take pride in their customs, language, food, and heritage. Young people were able to learn about their history through new multicultural school curricula and specialized departments in colleges, such as Asian or disabilities studies. As one indication of this, immigrants today tend to hold onto their ethnic names. Cindy Chang, a reporter for the *New York Times*, interviewed immigrants with difficult-to-pronounce names. Unlike past generations, these new immigrants do not want to Americanize their names. "They can't say my first name," said Naira Mnatsakanyan, an Armenian accounting student now living in California. "It's really hard for them. But I love for them to try and say it, since it's my name, it's my father's name."[4]

Finding an identity is a lifelong process, but it is an essential part of living a full life. Chicano labor organizer César Chávez, who cofounded the United Farm Workers (UFW) in the 1960s, believed that building up a people's pride is the key to changing their lives for the better. In the agricultural fields of California, Chávez found his fight for better working conditions for farmworkers was not unlike Dr. King's efforts to end segregation at lunch counters and city buses. "Once social change begins, it cannot be reversed. You cannot humiliate the person who feels pride. You cannot oppress the people who are not afraid anymore. The UFW was a beginning. We attacked a historical force of infamy . . . not by complaining, not by seeking handouts . . . we organized,"[5] said Chávez.

2

The Journey Up Gold Mountain

Shouting racial slurs, two white men attacked four Chinese American college students driving in a car in Queens, New York, one night in August 2006. Horrified neighbors shouted at them to stop as the men hurled racial slurs and then beat the victims, injuring them. The two men were arrested that night. Charges against them were elevated to a hate crime because of the racial epithets. A hate crime, first defined in the early 1980s, is motivated by prejudice against certain groups of people. Later, one of the victims told reporters, "They called me a stupid gook. They said it over and over again. . . . They did it because I am Asian."[6] The incident received intense attention from the press and politicians. Queens district attorney Richard A. Brown called it "a throwback to a dark time and place in American history and . . . an affront to civilized society."[7]

A few nights later, New York City councilman John C. Liu held a news conference with three of the victims. In 2006, Liu was the first and only Asian American to hold elected office in New York City, which has the second-largest Asian population of any U.S. city. He was elected to the city council in 2001 from the Queens neighborhood of Flushing, where streets are lined with Chinese and Korean supermarkets, video stores, and restaurants. Liu urged that the perpetrators be brought to justice. "We need a very swift and thorough response on the part of law enforcement," said Liu.[8]

The disturbing incident shows how far the Asian American community has come, and how far it still has to go. Once banned from citizenship and unable to own property, Asian Americans today are making themselves known and counted. Making up about 4 percent of the U.S. population, they are no longer hidden in Chinatowns or disenfranchised at the ballot box. They are an integral part of American society. The list of Asian American success stories and leaders in their fields is long: nuclear physicist and Nobel Prize winner Samuel Chao Chung Ting; the founder of Yahoo Jerry Yang; AIDS researcher David Ho; former secretary of Transportation Norman Yoshio Mineta; comedian Margaret Cho; Olympic skater Kristi Yamaguchi; and cellist Yo-Yo Ma, to name only a few. Asian bylines are common in major newspapers, and writers such as Amy Tan are on the best-seller lists. More Asians are voting, and hundreds are elected to public office every year, adding their voices to the political debate.

Yet Asian success has sometimes bred misunderstanding, fueling prejudice and hate crimes, such as the attacks on the Queens college students in 2006. Still, these incidents are no longer downplayed, instead attracting front-page attention and speedy prosecution. John C. Liu and other Asian politicians and advocacy groups step in to demand justice and policy changes. Still, the fact that such incidents occur shows that Asians face barriers. Language and cultural differences make it difficult for new immigrants to gain acceptance in American society. Stereotypes persist: In television and the movies, Asian actors are still cast as exotic strangers or treacherous martial arts experts. The so-called bamboo ceiling preventing people from advancing in some professions is still hard to crack; only a small number of Asians rise to top posts in corporations, academia, and other institutions.

Nevertheless, young people today are finding ways to integrate their Asian identities into modern American lives. Fareha Ahmed, a Pakistani American from New Jersey, rejected her parents' culture as a child, dying her hair blond and wearing hazel contact lenses. In college, with the support of good friends, she embraced her ethnicity. She introduced her roommates to Islamic holiday traditions and found "a good balance of East meets West,"[9] she told *Time* magazine.

FAST-GROWING AND DIVERSE

After Hispanics, Asian Americans are the second-fastest-growing immigrant group in the United States. Immigration from Asia increased by more than 45 percent in the 1990s. Approximately 11.9 million people, or 4.2 percent of the population, reported themselves as Asian or Asian and one or more other races, in the 2000 U.S. Census. Many are recent immigrants: more than half were born in Asia and immigrated to the United States. About 45 percent of these foreign-born Asians live in metropolitan areas of the major cities of Los Angeles, New York, and San Francisco. Asians now comprise 31 percent of the population in San Francisco; in New York City, Asians make up 11 percent of the city's residents. A few cities have an Asian majority, such as Daly City in the San Francisco Bay area with 51 percent of its population of Asian descent.

Unlike many identity groups, Asian Americans represent many cultures, ethnicities, languages, and religions. Asia is the largest continent and includes some 50 countries, including Pakistan, India, Japan, China, the Philippines,

South Korea, and Cambodia. When immigrants come to the United States, their differences sometimes seem greater than their similarities. Asian Americans include Japanese Americans who have lived in San Francisco for generations and Korean immigrants who have just settled in suburban New Jersey. In addition, Vietnam War refugees from rural Cambodia faced challenges unfamiliar to Indian doctors and engineers who immigrated to advance their professional careers.

Still, many Asian Americans have common bonds, and their cultures often share styles of food preparation, values, and certain attitudes. In many Asian cultures, the young respect the old, and families value hard work, self-discipline, and self-control. Asians from different countries are also linked through common religions: For example, the residents of Indonesia and Pakistan are predominately Muslim. Other religions, such as Buddhism and Taoism, are rooted in Asia. Asian American writer Maxine Hong Kingston sees the many similarities. She notes that Asians have similar family structures and kinship systems, and many of their languages are connected. Asians also come from a region that has been colonized and often marginalized by the West, she says. "There is the sense of being Easterners in a world where globalization has to do with Westernization,"[10] said Kingston in a National Public Radio interview.

"YELLOW PERIL"

Some of the bonds among Asian Americans were woven from experiences of discrimination and the sense of being "perpetual outsiders." The term *perpetual outsider* means that no matter how many generations their families have lived in the United States and have been U.S. citizens, they are still considered foreigners, identified by their country of origin. Frank H. Wu, dean of Wayne State University Law

School, is a second-generation Chinese American who is often asked, "Where are you really from?" When he replies that he is from Detroit, people still press him: "But where are you really from?" Finally, he says that his parents were born in China. Similarly, after a speech, people will come up to him to express surprise that he has no Chinese accent. "Once again, I have been mistaken for a foreigner or told I cannot be a real American,"[11] writes Wu in *Yellow: Race in America Beyond Black and White.*

Starting with the earliest Asian immigrants, these newcomers faced a precarious welcome that often turned hostile. The first major influx from Asia began when Chinese laborers sailed across the Pacific Ocean to join the California gold rush in the late 1840s. Fleeing famine and civil war, the Chinese men called California *Gum San* or "Gold Mountain" for its promise of prosperity. Full of hope and willing to work hard, the Chinese confronted prejudice and hostility. Made fun of for their blue pants and shirts, ethnic food, and traditional queues, or long single braids, Chinese workers could only pan for gold in streams already panned by white men. Starting in 1850, the Chinese had to pay a miner's tax that no other group had to pay. It was a huge expense for a gold miner. When the gold rush played out, the Chinese were hired to build the transcontinental railroad. Even as they worked hard, laws restricted them from becoming citizens, marrying whites, and owning of property. Chinese workers went on strike to win the right not to be whipped. In Denver, many Chinese were lynched. In 1882, Congress passed the Chinese Exclusion Act, banning Chinese laborers from entering the country. The law remained in effect for more than 60 years, until 1943.

Name-calling and negative stereotypes reflected the suspicion and distrust the Chinese encountered. "Yellow

After gold was discovered in California in 1848, the Chinese were one of many groups that came to the United States in search of fortune. Many of these newcomers were discriminated against, and the California legislature even passed a foreign miners tax to dissuade them from prospecting for gold. Here, two Chinese workers pan for gold in California around 1855.

peril" was a phrase coined by white Americans in the late nineteenth century to express fears that Chinese would invade with a foreign language and customs and take jobs from them. This fear was so prevalent that it extended to the courts. Supreme Court Justice John Marshall Harlan wrote in the case of *United States v. Wong Kim Ark* in 1898:

The presence within our territory of large numbers of Chinese laborers, of a distinct race and religion, remaining strangers in the land, residing apart by themselves, tenaciously adhering to the customs and usages of their own country, unfamiliar with our institutions and apparently incapable of assimilating with our people, might endanger good order, and be injurious to the public interests.[12]

Laws restricting specific nationalities and social classes of Asian immigrants continued to be imposed in the twentieth century. San Francisco segregated public schools to keep out Japanese children. Arizona banned immigrants from India. In 1910, an immigration station, Angel Island, opened in San Francisco Bay. Asian immigrants arriving from across the Pacific Ocean were held for months on Angel Island and then often forced to return to their native countries. Those immigrants who stayed were unable to become citizens. Asians could not vote, own property, or integrate into society. Forbidden to marry white Americans, they developed self-supporting communities, isolated from the mainstream. They lived, worked, and went to school in Chinatowns in large cities.

INTERNMENT CAMPS

Recruited to work on Hawaiian sugar plantations in the late 1800s, Japanese began immigrating to the mainland United States when their contracts expired. Many of them started as farmers on the West Coast, and then opened businesses and formed communities. Though they faced restrictive laws, nothing could compare to the animosity that erupted after the Japanese Navy bombed Pearl Harbor, Hawaii, on December 7, 1941. During this unprovoked and surprise attack, the Japanese bombed U.S. military and naval bases, installations, and ships at Pearl Harbor and at other locations in Hawaii.

The United States declared war against Japan and entered World War II. Japanese Americans were suddenly considered dangerous enemies who might be spies or betray the United States. In February 1942, President Franklin D. Roosevelt signed Executive Order 9066, which allowed the government to remove Japanese Americans from their homes and send them to internment camps set up in remote areas. The order permitted the secretary of the army to designate large parts of the country as military areas and to "exclude," or keep out, certain people from those areas, mainly Japanese Americans. About one-third of the country was deemed a military area, including much of the West. Japanese in California, Oregon, and other states were rounded up and taken away. "For the first time in 81 years, not a single Japanese is walking the streets of San Francisco,"[13] the *San Francisco Chronicle* reported on May 21, 1942. People of Japanese descent had been "humanely" evacuated for the safety of the country and themselves, the *Chronicle* declared. Their businesses were seized and family possessions were stored.

Not even the Supreme Court was concerned about the possible violation of civil rights of detainees who were neither charged nor convicted of crimes. In two major cases involving the Japanese internment, the Supreme Court condoned the process. In all, some 120,000 Japanese men, women, and children were interned for up to four years during World War II. They were housed in internment camps, surrounded by barbed wire and armed guards, in the barren Arizona desert and other remote areas. About half the internees were children. They were forced to live in crude overcrowded housing, without good sanitation, and to survive on rations.

Actor George Takei, who played Mr. Sulu on the *Star Trek* television show, was five years old when his family was taken to an internment camp. He quickly got used to the barbed wire and sentry guards carrying machine guns. As a child, he did not understand where he was and why he was there. "It wasn't until we came out that we realized that it was something like a jail and only bad people go to jail—so there must be something bad about being a Japanese American and you grow up feeling ashamed of who you are,"[14] Takei told the BBC in 2006. Though many leaders later expressed regret about these events, more than 40 years passed before President Ronald Reagan signed the Civil Liberties Act of 1988, providing a redress, or payment, of $20,000 to each detainee still alive.

"YELLOW POWER"

Until the mid-1960s, immigration from Asia was severely limited. A 1952 law restricted Asian immigration to fewer than 3,000 people a year, compared with 150,000 Europeans. Elected in 1960, President John F. Kennedy wanted to improve relations with Asia. He worked toward a new immigration law to reach out to Asia, but he was assassinated before it was passed. President Lyndon Johnson signed the Immigration and Nationality Act of 1965, also known as the Hart-Celler Act, which abolished quotas by national origin. Under the new law, immigrants were allowed to enter the United States because of their skills and professions. The law also favored the reunification of families. Asian Americans began bringing parents, sisters and brothers, and other relatives. The population grew rapidly, becoming more diverse, as immigrants arrived from India, Taiwan, the Philippines, and many other countries. After the Vietnam War ended in 1975, millions of Southeast Asians from Cambodia, Vietnam, and Laos fled to the United States.

The influx of Asians coincided with the civil rights movement and antiwar protests of the 1960s and 1970s. Inspired by the identity movements of blacks and other minorities, Asian students at Princeton, Yale, San Francisco State College, and the University of California, Berkeley took to the streets, shouting "Yellow Power" and "Yellow is Beautiful." In 1968, Berkeley students held up a banner that stated, "Asian Americans for Justice," during a rally in support of Black Panther Huey Newton. Like other identity groups, Asians pressed for recognition, respect, and civil rights. They wanted to empower their communities and gain understanding from the larger society. California students went on strike to demand that Asian studies departments be established at universities. In response, departments devoted to Asian history, culture, and literature were set up at major universities, including Berkeley.

Asian activists emerged on many fronts. They drew San Francisco's attention to the impoverished conditions in the city's neglected Chinatown. Student activist Jeffrey Paul Chan and his friends published the first anthology of Asian American literature in 1974, *Aiiieeeee! An Anthology of Asian American Writers*. Lawyers formed organizations, such as the Asian Law Caucus, and pursued cases involving civil rights. A class-action suit was brought against a national insurance company for discriminating against Asians in hiring practices; another was launched against the San Francisco Police Department for employing a dragnet or mass arrests of youths in Chinatown. To address the mental health needs of the community, the Asian American Psychological Association was founded in 1972. In addition, business, arts, and science organizations focused on many facets of the Asian American identity.

To organize as Asian Americans, different communities, such as the Chinese and Japanese, had to put aside deep-seated antagonisms and cultural and language differences. Sometimes, only a crisis could bridge the gaps. This happened in 1982 in Detroit, Michigan, when Vincent Chin, a Chinese-American engineer, was attacked in a bar and later on the

Established in the 1850s, San Francisco's Chinatown is the oldest and largest of its kind in the United States. Unfortunately, by the early 1970s, the neighborhood had become run down and was in dire need of revitalization. Here, Chinese Americans cross a Chinatown street in December 1971.

street by two autoworkers who mistook him for Japanese. One of them had been laid off, and they blamed Chin for the downturn in the automobile industry due to Japanese auto imports. Chin died of his injuries. Chinese Americans were joined by Korean, Japanese, and other communities in expressing their outrage when the two men received only probation and a small fine as punishment. They formed American Citizens for Justice—one of the first Asian-American organizations spanning ethnic lines—to fight against hate crimes. (Laws against hate crimes were first proposed by the Anti-Defamation League, an organization established to combat anti-Semitism, in the early 1980s.)

Names do matter, as identity movements have asserted. Until the 1960s, people of Asian ancestry were called "Oriental," a remnant of a past when Western colonists ruled Asian nations. In the early 1970s, the term *Asian American* was picked up by academics, journalists, and, eventually, the public. The federal government created an Asian American population category for the census and other official documents. Today, the identity group usually includes Pacific Islanders, such as Hawaiians, under the name Asian Pacific Americans, or just APA. People often identify themselves simply as Asians.

THE MODEL MINORITY

Many Asian Americans have indeed achieved success. In 2006, the average median income of Asian Americans was $61,094. This average was higher than any group, including whites, according to the U.S. Census Bureau. Asians as a group also make their mark in academics. In 2007, the New York City Department of Education reported that Asian-American students comprised 62 percent of the student body at the highly competitive Stuyvesant High School in New York City, a public school where admission is based on merit and not race. According to the University of California, at state campuses in California, Asian Americans made up 35 percent of the admitted freshmen in 2007, compared to 3.6 percent African Americans, 18.7 percent Latinos, and 35.5 percent whites.

In 1966, sociologist William Peterson wrote "Success Story: Japanese-American Style" for the *New York Times Magazine*. He used the term *model minority* to describe Japanese Americans, whom he characterized as having risen from marginalization to become successful, law-abiding citizens. By the 1990s, the model minority was a popular stereotype for all Asian Americans, but many people refer to the description as the "model minority myth." On the one hand, the label describes Asians as high-achieving, family-oriented, hard-working, and responsible citizens. Typecast as straight-A students, excelling in math and music, Asian students are not expected to excel at sports. In addition, Asian entrepreneurs and professionals are stereotypically seen as industrious perfectionists.

Some Asians fit some of these stereotypes, but many do not. Critics say the model minority tag sets unrealistic expectations for a varied population. Not all Asian children breeze through calculus and chemistry. Some struggle in the classroom. The label ignores the new immigrants and the elderly who do not speak English, lack job skills, and live in poverty. In some cities, gangs have attracted young people who have few other options. A 2006 report by California State University, Sacramento on Asian American and Pacific Islanders in Sacramento, California, found that 25 percent live under the federal poverty level of $20,000 for a family of four.[15] Many of those Asians living in poverty are refugees from Vietnam and Laos, whereas Japanese Americans in Sacramento are generally more affluent. As this study shows, Asians are as diverse as any large group of people.

The model minority label has other negative effects. Sometimes the sense that Asians are so successful has caused a backlash, particularly in times of economic stress. "Material success has bred resentment, envy, even backlashes of violence from such other subnationalities as blacks and Latinos,"[16] writes James Walsh in *Time* magazine. The label also ignores the language and cultural barriers, racism, and bigotry that Asian Americans still encounter. The assumption that Asians can do it on their own makes the government more reluctant to offer services to those in need. Another negative effect of the stereotype is its implication that Asians are quiet and submissive. In other words, they do not get involved in politics. In fact, the numbers of Asian American voters are growing every year.

"OUR VOICE IS OUR VOTE"

At a recent election rally in Little Saigon, a Vietnamese neighborhood in Orange County, California, Vietnamese American residents held up signs that read, "Today we rally. Tomorrow we vote" and "Our Voice is Our Vote."[17] It was October 2006, and they were gathered to listen to candidates running for office. These voters are part of a phenomenon that one recent study called a "sleeping giant" awakening in California and througout the country. Between 2000 and 2005, a half million new Asian American voters registered in California alone. In coming years, Asian Americans "will likely have a significant impact on state and national politics,"[18] predicted Don Nakanishi, director of UCLA's Asian American Studies Center, which released the report in 2006.

It has been a long road. Asians had to overcome a history of limited participation in politics, due partly to their long delay in gaining citizenship rights. Chinese were not allowed to become citizens until 1943; Asian Indians could not vote until 1946; and Japanese Americans were restricted from citizenship until 1952. This sense of being an outsider lingered, making immigrants reluctant to vote even when they became citizens. Language barriers and isolation in communities where politicians rarely ventured also impeded participation in politics. Gradually, Asian politicians sought office and were elected. Dalip Singh Saund was born in a small village in India in 1899. He immigrated to the United States in 1920 to study at the University of California, Berkeley. Saund became a citizen in 1949, and in 1956, he became the first Asian elected to the U.S. House of

In recent years, Asian Americans have become more politically active, especially in California. For example, between 2000 and 2005, more than half a million Asian Americans registered to vote in California. Here, Senator Hillary Rodham Clinton (D-New York) speaks at a gathering of the Asian American and Pacific Islanders for Hillary for President in Washington, D.C., in May 2007.

Representatives, representing California. In 1959, the same year Hawaii became a state, Hawaiians elected businessman and lawyer Hiram Leong Fong as the first Asian U.S. senator. Hawaii's Daniel K. Inouye became a powerful presence in the U.S. Senate through eight terms, starting in 1963. In 1965, the first Asian American woman in Congress, Patsy Takemoto Mink, of Hawaii, went to Washington, D.C. Meanwhile, Asian Americans took office in cities and states throughout the country. In 2004, a total number of 346 Asian Americans were elected to federal, state, and local positions compared to 120 in 1978, according to the Asian American Justice Center, an advocacy group.

Efforts to boost the Asian vote have grown in recent years. On one front, advocates want to ensure that Section

FROM A LAOTIAN VILLAGE TO THE STATE HOUSE

Mee Moua was born in a small Hmong village in Laos, but she does not remember much of her early childhood. She was five years old when her family fled Laos after the Communist takeover following the Vietnam War. They spent five years in a refugee camp in Thailand. Finally, the family was resettled in the United States. They moved to a public housing complex in Appleton, Wisconsin, where many Hmong immigrants from the mountains of northern Laos had been resettled. Moua recalls feeling alienated from the predominately white Catholic community. "Church people would show up at our house on Christmas with trees and stuff, but there were also people who spit at us and called us chinks, gooks and told us to go home,"* she remembered in a PBS interview. Many Hmong adults could not read or write in their native language, or speak English, and they found it difficult to assimilate. They kept to themselves and did not mix with the local community. The prejudice she encountered made her cling more to her Hmong identity, but Moua was determined to get an education and have a career.

Moua graduated from Brown University and received a master's degree from the University of Texas, before attending the University of Minnesota Law School. She was in her early 30s when she turned her aspirations to politics. In 2002, Mee Moua was elected to the Minnesota State House, becoming the first Hmong American legislator in the

203 of the Voting Rights Act of 1965, which was renewed for 25 more years in 2006, is followed in neighborhoods with large non-English speaking populations. Section 203 requires language assistance, such as Asian-language ballots and interpreters, in areas where a minority group has more than 10,000 people or 5 percent of the voting-age population. Unfortunately, there are gaps in services. A national study "Sound Barriers: Asian Americans and Language Access in Election 2004" by Asian advocacy groups found that language

country. One of her first efforts in office was to push for a bill to legalize traditional Hmong marriage ceremonies. Surprisingly, some of the opponents to the bill were from the Hmong community, and she eventually had to drop the bill. Moua realized that treading the line between communities was not going to be easy.

Still, Moua has a wide base of support, not just from Hmong but from others in her district, as well. When running for reelection in 2006, her long list of endorsements spanned groups representing firefighters, nurses, teachers, farmworkers, and environmentalists. Moua, who is married with two children, feels most strongly about issues that are shared by all her constituents: jobs, education, transportation, and support for soldiers and veterans. The Hmong community has also come a long way. Moua is a member of the Hmong Bar Association, composed of Minnesota lawyers from the Hmong community. She is a prime example of an Asian-American politician who is looking out for her community at home, while moving up in American politics. "The issue is not whether Asian American politicians are ready; it's really whether America is ready,"** she told PBS.

---

* "Asian American Politicians: Mee Moua." Searching for Asian America, PBS.org, 2004. Available online at *http://www.pbs.org/searching/aap_mmoua.html*
** Ibid.

barriers remain a significant obstacle to immigrants. In voting districts covered by federal voting rights laws and requiring language assistance and bilingual materials, many Asian voters could not find bilingual materials or the poll workers were unwilling to help them, the report stated.[19]

Other efforts are aimed at unifying the Asian vote, often split between Republican and Democrat. The 80-20 Initiative is a national nonpartisan group trying to increase the clout of Asian voters. The group encourages Asians to vote as a block in favor of candidates of any party that supports Asian issues, such as prosecuting discrimination, lifting the glass ceiling (preventing minorities from obtaining upper-level posotions within a company), and appointing Asian Americans to government jobs. Local initiatives are also underway. Filipino Americans in Hawaii in 2006 reached across party lines to get people to the polls and push for a Filipino voting block. They took practical measures such as multilingual voter outreach and registration. Filipinos comprise about 15 percent of Hawaii's population, but many do not vote, and none have been elected to Congress. "We recognize that there are a lot of Filipino voters who are intimidated by the voting machines, and afraid that they won't be able to operate them when they get to the polls," said one Democratic activist. "And even that very simple matter, but a major deterrent to the electoral participation, will be addressed."[20] The next step is electing more Asians in districts not predominately Asian. For example, in 1998, David Wu was elected to Congress from Portland, Oregon, not a heavily Asian district. Wu, who emigrated from China as a child, was still the first and only Chinese American in the House of Representatives when he won a fourth term in 2004.

POKÉMON AND MANGA

In 1979, President Jimmy Carter set aside a week in May as Asian Pacific American Heritage Week. The celebration of Asian culture and contributions was expanded to the month of May in 1992. Today, American pop culture is filled with Asian images, products, and ideas. From kung fu movies to Hello Kitty toys, Asian products clearly appeal to young Americans. Pre-teenagers trade Pokémon cards, and adolescents buy books of Manga, the Japanese comics, from the chain bookstores. J-Rock, Japanese rock music, also crossed the Pacific and found adherents throughout the globe. The Indian tradition of yoga is part of many Americans' daily regime, while Indian-inspired women's fashions fill the malls. Eating at a Thai restaurant or wearing an Indian silk blouse does not necessarily increase understanding between cultures, however. "We forget that people can eat Asian foods but still have contempt for Asian people,"[21] writes Frank Wu.

The phrase "Asian Pride" is used by young people today to celebrate their Asian heritage. "Got Rice?" a spin-off from the famous milk ad "Got Milk?" became popular in the 1990s as a humorous way to show solidarity among young Asians, even spawning a rap song. Still, many young people are caught between their heritage and life in the United States. They struggle to define themselves and where they fit in the world. Should they call themselves Chinese American, Asian American, or just American? Does being Asian American take away from their ethnicity? In the book of essays *Asian American X*, edited by Arar Han and John Hsu, young writers describe their search for identity. They talk about being called "Gook" and "Chink" in elementary school and only hanging out with Asian students in high school. Some rejected their parents' customs but did not feel comfortable in the white mainstream either. Matthew Noerper was born to Korean parents and adopted by a white American family. "I hesitate to even call myself Asian American,"[22] writes Noerper, who never felt comfortable in either world. As the writers relate, each person's journey toward identity is different. Some travel to the country of their grandparents and became fluent in the language. Others study their ancestral country in college, learning about Korea or India for the first time. Still others become immersed in American culture and turn away from their Asian roots, at least temporarily.

The search for identity is a lifelong challenge for many Asian Americans, even for John C. Liu, the city councilman from Queens. Liu was five years old when he moved with his family from Taiwan, and his father changed his name from Chun to John after John F. Kennedy. He grew up in New York and attended college. He does not speak Mandarin, and he needs a translator when he speaks with constituents. "There are non-Asians who look at me and see an Asian, and there are Asians who look at me and see an American,"[23] he told the *New York Times* in 2006. Even so, he says, his position as the first Asian to hold office in New York City is a responsibility he happily accepts. He says, "There's a lot of pressures that come along with it, but also lots of opportunity."[24]

3

The Disability Rights Movement

All Edward V. Roberts wanted to do was to attend the University of California, Berkeley. He was accepted, and there was no reason why he could not go, except it was the early 1960s, and Roberts, who was paralyzed from the neck down after a bout with polio, used a wheelchair. At that time, a person who used a wheelchair faced obstacles in every part of daily life, from doors that would not open wide enough to steps that were too high and desks that were too low. As a result, Roberts and millions of others were denied basic freedoms that most people take for granted. They could not board buses and subways. They could not go to work. Roberts could not live in a dorm room or get up the steps to classes.

Instead of giving up, Roberts decided to fight for his right to attend the university of his choice. He talked with university administrators, and they made accommodations so he could attend classes. Reflecting the attitudes of the era, a local newspaper printed an article entitled "Helpless cripple attends UC classes." Roberts went on to become the director of the California Department of Rehabilitation and the cofounder and director of the Center for Independent Living in Berkeley, two leading organizations that have helped integrate people with disabilities into American society.

Roberts was a pioneer in the disability rights movement, a grassroots campaign that started a revolution for people with disabilities. More than 54 million people in the United States are living with a disability, according to the U.S. Census Bureau. *Disability* is defined as a condition that interferes with major life activities, such as talking, walking, hearing, seeing, working, or caring for one's self. Disabilities may be physical or cognitive and can include spinal cord injury, multiple sclerosis, brain injury, alcoholism, HIV/AIDS, polio, schizophrenia, and hundreds of other conditions. Some disabilities are genetic and are present at birth, while others are caused by unforeseen circumstances during a person's life. Disability "is the one minority anyone can join at any time, as a result of a sudden automobile accident, a fall down a flight of stairs, cancer or disease,"[25] writes journalist Joseph P. Shapiro, an expert on disability rights. In fact, one-third of the elderly have a disability, so no one is immune from the possibility. Thus, the issues of the disabled are shared by all of society.

"OUT OF SIGHT, OUT OF MIND"

Not very long ago, people with disabilities were treated with pity, disgust, or misunderstanding. They were seen as people who could not make decisions for themselves, so others made decisions for them. Prejudice against people with disabilities was common, resulting in name-calling, housing discrimination, and warehousing in institutions. "Out of sight, out of mind" was the practice. People with severe disabilities were locked away in hospitals and kept for years in nursing homes, unable to learn life skills or receive job training, and separated from their families, homes, and communities where there was no support for them anyway. Those individuals who "overcame" their disabilities were considered heroic; others who struggled were seen as pitable.

However change was on the horizon, and it would come from disabled people who knew what they wanted and needed. The disability rights movement has been led by the disabled themselves. "Nothing about us, without us," is a common refrain. They set out to change social attitudes, often through direct action and nonviolent protest. They rolled wheelchairs down the streets of New York City and staged sit-ins in federal offices. They lobbied their senators and filed lawsuits. They wanted respect, not sympathy. Rather than be viewed as sick or suffering from medical problems, the disabled wanted to be seen as a group of people who enjoyed the same civil rights and freedoms as anyone else. Even medical advances did not always help. "There are people with serious spinal cord injuries who used to die within two weeks that now live 30 or 40 years. It's one thing to say we have this marvelous technology, but if nobody's going to hire you, what's the point?"[26] said Dr. Frank Bowe, a deaf scholar and disability rights activist who wrote *Handicapping America* in 1978.

Most important, disability activists wanted access and reasonable accommodations so that they could live up to their potential. Their disabilities were not the problem; instead, it was the building that did not have ramps and the school that did not have a qualified teacher to address a child's learning issues. By removing obstacles and gaining simple tools, such as attendant care or wheelchair ramps, they would not need the handouts and sympathy that had been the norm for so long.

SEEDS OF CHANGE

The seeds of the disability rights movement were sown in the nineteenth century. In 1817, Thomas Hopkins Gallaudet, a Congregational minister whose neighbor's child was deaf, opened the American School for the Deaf in Hartford, Connecticut; it was the first school for children with a disability. Until then, deaf children were unable to get an education. Connecticut governor Oliver Wolcott was impressed, and asked the public for support "in elevating the condition of a class of mankind who have been heretofore considered as incapable of mental improvement, but who are now found to be susceptible of instruction in various arts and sciences."[27] Soon, schools to educate blind children were begun, as well. The Perkins School for the Blind opened in Boston in 1832. New attention was given to people with other disabilities. Dorothea Dix, a prominent New England social reformer and teacher, took on the cause of the mentally ill. Mental illness was considered a hopeless condition, and families turned out their relatives with mental illness. People were often left to survive in jails and poorhouses. In 1841, Dix was teaching women inmates at the East Cambridge jail and saw mentally ill inmates neglected and freezing in cold, bare rooms with only straw to sleep on. Dix started a crusade to establish hospitals for the mentally ill, where they could be cared for humanely.

As the nineteenth century progressed, more educational opportunities became available to people with disabilities. In 1864, a small school for deaf children in Washington, D.C., was turned into a college. President Abraham Lincoln signed the bill allowing the school to confer college degrees. The college eventually became Gallaudet University, a world-renowned liberal arts college for the deaf and hard of hearing that was named after Thomas Hopkins Gallaudet. At the same time, Alexander Graham Bell, the inventor of the telephone, opened a school for the deaf in Northampton, Massachusetts, which focused on oral tradition, teaching the students to speak.

After World War I, disabled veterans returned home in large numbers, unable to work because of missing limbs or other injuries. They needed jobs, and the country needed them to be independent. In 1918, a vocational rehabilitation program for veterans was established to help them retrain and gain marketable skills. The idea was expanded in 1920, when President Woodrow Wilson signed into law a national vocational rehabilitation program. Not just veterans but also civilians with disabilities became eligible for job counseling and training, prosthetics (if they were missing a limb), and job-placement services. For the first time, the U.S. government took responsibility for helping people with disabilities enter the workforce. Today, vocational rehabilitation is more comprehensive and may include education, career counseling, and other services.

Yet attitudes toward the disabled were slow to change. Franklin D. Roosevelt contracted polio in 1921, when he was 39 years old. The viral disease left him paralyzed from the waist down. Well aware of the public's fears about disabilities, Roosevelt strove to hide his paralysis and kept searching for a cure. Elected governor of New York after his bout with polio, he never appeared in public in a wheelchair. Although Roosevelt was the first president to use a wheelchair when he was elected in 1932, he hid the extent of his disability. Instead, he pushed forward legislation for more rehabilitation services for all people with disabilities. "We know that there is nothing wrong with the spirit of these people, but without special assistance they may become a social as well as an economic liability,"[28] he said.

After World War II, parents began a grassroots movement to provide a brighter future for children with disabilities. Parents started to demand better services and living conditions for their children with mental retardation, many of whom were housed in state institutions. Their

During his term as governor of New York, Franklin D. Roosevelt hid the fact that he was paralyzed from the waist down. Even after he was elected president in 1932, the extent of his paralysis was kept secret, because people with disabilities were often looked down upon. Here, Roosevelt talks to Ruthie Bie, the granddaughter of the local caretaker, at his home in Hyde Park, New York, in 1941.

efforts not only helped to initiate new community services and education and employment opportunities for people with disabilities but also inspired others to realize that they could speak out and make a difference. In 1962, President John F. Kennedy, whose sister Rosemary was mentally retarded, started the President's Panel on Mental Retardation to address many of these difficult issues.

LIVING INDEPENDENTLY

By the 1960s and 1970s, a new determination took hold among the disabled to press for equal rights and opportunities, much as the civil rights and women's movements had begun to achieve. The first waves came in California, where advocates, including Edward V. Roberts, started the independent living movement, an effort to give people the skills and support system to live on their own. Until then, for many people with disabilities, the possibility of living in the community was not possible. Instead, they were housed, and sometimes neglected, in state institutions and not given the tools or opportunities to gain life skills. In his book *No Pity: People with Disabilities Forging a New Civil Rights Movement*, Joseph P. Shapiro recounts the story of a bright young man with cerebral palsy whose mother sent him to a nursing home after she was unable to lift him into his wheelchair, even though he had the potential to live at home with a little extra help. Advocates for the disabled realized that even those people with severe disabilities could live in the community, if they were provided with support services and life skills training. Not only would this help them live fuller lives, but the costs to society would lessen, too.

In the early 1970s, disability activists opened the first Center for Independent Living in Berkeley. Staffed by health and social services professionals, the center offered assistance to disabled clients to get them into housing and to provide social services, financial assistance, and advocacy advice. Soon, independent living centers were opening throughout the country. Today, there are approximately 680 nonprofit centers in 50 states, some receiving public funding. Offering a mixture of support and advocacy, many centers use a peer approach: People with disabilities show others how they go about their daily lives. The Boston Center for Independent Living was one of the first centers, founded by local activists in 1974. It acts as a civil rights organization by providing advocacy, information, and support to people with disabilities. In 2006, the center won a major class-action lawsuit against the Metropolitan Boston Transit Authority (MBTA), requiring the bus and subway system to upgrade escalators and elevators, buy new low-floor buses, improve public address systems, and make other improvements to assist disabled passengers.

In the 1970s, advocates for the disabled had a long way to go. New civil rights laws had to be written. Funding had to be set aside for services and accommodations, from bus lifts to sign-language interpreters. During the years since the 1970s, some 50 laws have been passed to protect the civil rights and freedoms of the disabled. The root of the laws has been the right to equal access: In other words, people with disabilities had the right to ride buses, attend school, go to work, take out a library book, and engage in everyday American life.

SECTION 504

"They're tired, they're grubby, they're uncomfortable . . . but their spirits are soaring. . . . The water has been turned off on the fourth floor, where the occupation army of cripples has taken over."[29] That was a reporter's account of a historic sit-in that took place in San Francisco in April 1977. Approximately 125 people with disabilities, many in wheelchairs, took over the federal building at 50 Fulton Street. They refused to leave until the government agreed to enforce the first major law to protect the disabled from discrimination. Throughout the nation in other cities, similar sit-ins were taking place.

Nearly four years earlier, Congress passed the Rehabilitation Act of 1973, which provided federal funds for services to people with disabilities. Though civil rights laws passed in the 1960s protected other minority groups, people with disabilities were left out. In fact, the Rehabilitation Act had taken years to pass. President Richard Nixon refused to sign a similar bill in 1970. Following Nixon's snub, disability rights protestors stopped traffic in cities throughout the country to convince Congress to override two presidential vetoes. Although the bill was close to being passed, some of it's wording troubled policy makers. Known as Section 504, it bans discrimination because of disability by institutions, employers, or organizations that received federal funds. It reads in part: "No other qualified individual with a disability in the United States . . . shall solely by reason of her or his handicap be excluded from participation in, be denied the benefits of, or be subjected to discrimination under any program or activity receiving Federal financial assistance." Modeled after earlier civil rights laws banning discrimination on the basis of sex, race, and ethnic origin, Section 504 marked the first federal civil rights law for the disabled.

Yet, three years later, Section 504 had stalled. Critics in the government were dragging their feet, worried that the cost of implementing the law was too high. They refused to write regulations to put it in place. Along with other activists, the American Coalition of Citizens with Disabilities (ACCD), an advocacy organization, decided to make Section 504 a priority. At the time, Frank Bowe was the leader of the ACCD. Bowe, who is deaf, was trained as a psychologist and became a leader in the disability rights movement. He organized sit-ins in 10 cities during the spring of 1977 to urge the government to come up with rules to enforce the law. In San Francisco, demonstrators refused to leave the offices at the U.S. Department of Health, Education, and Welfare for 28 days. People in wheelchairs sang "We Shall Not Be Moved" and carried signs that read: "504 Human Rights for All." Finally, in May 1977, Secretary of Health, Education, and Welfare Joseph Califano approved the regulations, and Section 504 went into effect.

However, major battles still lay ahead. Even though Section 504 protected the disabled from discrimination in federally funded programs, no protections existed in the private sector. Thus, people with disabilities who worked for private businesses or wanted to get services in hotels, restaurants, and stores still had no right to access or reasonable accommodations. A much broader law was needed.

AMERICANS WITH DISABILITIES ACT

People in wheelchairs with disabilities still could not ride buses, subways, and other transportation. Most public transportation systems lacked any accommodations for wheelchairs or other assistive devices. This was because the government had allowed public transportation systems to bypass Section 504 with less expensive alternative transportation, known as paratransit, rather than adapt the regular buses or subways to accommodate people with disabilities. The paratransit vans were geographically limited and did not run very often, making it difficult for people to get to work, visit friends, and go shopping.

A group of disability activists in Denver, Colorado, calling themselves American Disabled for Accessible Public Transit (ADAPT), set out to make public transportation accessible. ADAPT activists blocked traffic, chained themselves to buses, and staged sit-ins at bus stops throughout the country. In early September 1988, police arrested dozens of demonstrators blocking Greyhound terminals throughout the country. In Dallas, Texas, five protestors in wheelchairs and a blind person were arrested.

In 1990, Congress passed the Americans with Disabilities Act, which was subsequently signed into law by President George H. W. Bush on July 26 of that year. The civil rights law prohibited discrimination on the basis of disability in employment, public services, public accommodations, and telecommunications. Here, wheelchair-bound demonstrators block Greyhound buses from entering a bus terminal shortly before the bus company agreed to install wheelchair lifts in 1995.

"Black people fought for the right to ride at the front of the bus. We're fighting for the right to get on the bus,"[30] said ADAPT organizer Mark Johnson.

They needed a federal law that would require buses to install lifts. Finally, in 1988, a bill that would become the Americans with Disabilities Act began to emerge in Congress. For two years, Congress and advocates debated the bill and made compromises. The momentum seemed to favor the disability rights advocates, who now had friends in Washington. Many legislators realized that the time had come to break down the barriers that kept the disabled from full participation in society.

In September 1989, Senator Tom Harkin (D-Iowa) stood before the Senate chamber to introduce the bill to his fellow senators. The son of a coal miner, Harkin's late brother, Frank, was deaf. Growing up in a small town in Iowa, Harkin learned sign language to communicate with his brother. He also grew to appreciate the obstacles his brother and others faced with disabilities faced. As a legislator in Washington, first a representative and then a senator starting in 1984, Harkin sought to improve the lives of people with disabilities. Together with Senator Bob Dole (R-Kansas) whose right arm was paralyzed by a war injury during World War II, Harkin coauthored the Senate version of the Americans with Disabilities Act. On the day he introduced it to the Senate, Harkin used sign language to communicate. "For too long individuals with disabilities have been excluded, segregated and otherwise denied equal, effective and meaningful opportunity to participate in the economic and social mainstream of American life," said Harkin. "It is time we eliminated these injustices."[31]

Signed into law on July 26, 1990, by President George H. W. Bush, the Americans with Disabilities Act (ADA) is a landmark civil rights law for people with disabilities. The act bans discrimination based on a person's disabilities and guarantees equal rights for people with disabilities in transportation, public accommodations, commercial facilities, employment, government services, and telecommunications. The ADA marked a turning point for people with disabilities, but often they still had to go to court to win the rights guaranteed under the new law. Here are two examples.

As a teenager in Oregon, Casey Martin was a promising golf player, winning many junior tournaments, but in college he was diagnosed with a circulatory disorder, Klippel-

Trenaunay-Webber syndrome, that weakened his right leg. As a member of the golf team at Stanford University, Martin had to ride a golf cart to get around the 18-hole course. After graduation, he became a professional golfer, but the PGA Tour had a rule against golf carts and refused to make an exception for Martin. PGA officials said that walking the course was one of the skills required to play the game. Martin filed suit on the basis of the ADA in 1997. His case went all the way to the Supreme Court, which ruled in a 7 to 2 majority in 2001 that he could use the golf cart.

In another case, a toddler, Jeremy Alvarez, who needed an inhaler for his asthma, found himself at odds with his prospective preschool, which had a "no medications" policy. If he had an asthma attack at school, he would have to wait for his parents or grandparents to bring his inhaler. His parents, Jose and Lynn Alvarez, were forced to choose between sending their son to school without his inhaler or finding a new school. They filed an ADA lawsuit, and the Department of Justice supported them, maintaining that the school had to make a few reasonable accommodations for the boy. The district court sided with the parents. The boy was allowed to bring his inhaler to school.

GOING TO SCHOOL

Helping children with disabilities to receive an appropriate education has been a priority of the disability rights movement. Judith Heumann, who contracted polio when she was a toddler, experienced discrimination as a young child. When she tried to enroll in public school, she was told that her wheelchair was a fire hazard. She was not able to go to school until fourth grade. Later, when she applied for teaching jobs in the New York City public schools, she was again told that it was not possible. She had to sue the school system in order to get a job. Heumann went on to

Washington, D.C. As legislative assistant to the chairperson of the Senate Committee on Labor and Public Welfare, Heumann helped develop landmark legislation now known as the Individuals with Disabilities Education Act (IDEA), first passed in 1975. This important law guarantees that students with disabilities receive a free and appropriate education in the least restrictive environment. The law requires schools to provide learning aids, classroom accommodations, and other measures to ensure students can learn. Heumann later became assistant secretary to the U.S. Department of Education, where she helped develop the Americans with Disabilities Act.

Still, students must often work hard to get the services they feel they need. Desiree Sheehy, a seven-year-old who lives in Franklin Lakes, New Jersey, asked to use a walker several hours a day in her public school classroom. She has a degenerative muscle condition that keeps her in a wheelchair, but for a few hours a day, she uses a walker to help build her strength. "In all my dreams, I've always wanted to walk," Desiree told the *Bergen Record*. "Whenever I have a dream I'm not in my wheelchair, I'm walking by myself."[32] School officials felt the walker was a burden for teachers to manage and stated that they provided other physical therapy instead. The school district refused to allow the walker, a decision that Desiree's family was appealing in the spring of 2007.

"DEAF PRESIDENT NOW"

Like any large group of people, those with disabilities are diverse, with many different needs. An adult who uses a wheelchair has different challenges than a child with autism or a senior citizen with visual impairments. The deaf community is one identity group that forged its own path. Starting in the late 1960s, advocates in the deaf community began to redefine deafness. Rather than viewing deafness as a disability, they saw it as a language difference. The first language of the deaf community is American Sign Language. The deaf community demanded the right to communicate through sign language and to determine their own culture and lifestyle. In 1988, this drive for self-determination and empowerment played out at Gallaudet University, the university for the deaf and hard of hearing in Washington, D.C.

Since Gallaudet was founded in 1864, the school was led by presidents who were not deaf. Students now wanted a deaf president who could share their experiences. When they learned that the Board of Trustees chose a new president who was not deaf, the students went on strike.

In 1988, Dr. I. King Jordan became Gallaudet University's first deaf president. The Washington, D.C., school is the only one in the world in which all of its programs and services are catered to students who are deaf or hard of hearing. Here, King speaks in sign during commencement exercises in May 2006, seven months before he stepped down as president.

COCHLEAR IMPLANTS: HOPE AND CONTROVERSY

New technology to allow deaf people to hear has raised both hope and controversy. Considered a miracle to some, the technology is criticized by others in the deaf community, who say the devices rob them of their identity. Cochlear implants are small electronic devices that can provide a sense of sound to people with hearing loss. Part of the device is surgically implanted beneath the skin; another part sits behind the ear. Unlike hearing aids, they do not make sounds louder, but electronically stimulate the auditory nerve, which sends signals to the brain. The process is not the same as normal hearing, and the person has to be trained to decipher the sounds. Only some people benefit from the implants, depending on the cause and severity of their deafness, but those who do may be able to hear the telephone, have conversations, listen to music, and learn in regular classrooms.

By 2005, nearly 100,000 people throughout the world had cochlear implants, according to the Federal Drug Administration. Yet the technology has ignited debate, raising questions about what it means to be deaf. For many in the deaf culture, deafness is not a problem that needs to be fixed. Rather, deafness is an identity like race or ethnicity, and the deaf are a language minority whose first language is American

The student protest was called "Deaf President Now." The protest lasted a week, and the students gained widespread attention and support from deaf advocates. The university listened to the students' demands. Dr. I. King Jordan, a respected deaf scholar, became Gallaudet's eighth president and the first who was deaf. Soon afterward, federal laws recognizing the needs of deaf citizens were passed. The Television Accessibility Enhancement Act required that televisions be accessible to people with hearing loss and established a national relay system for telecommunications devices for the deaf.

Sign Language (ASL). "In some ways, you're saying deaf people are not good enough, they need to be fixed. I don't need to be fixed. My brain works fine,"[*] signed Joshua Walker in an interview with the *New York Times*. Walker is a student at Gallaudet University. Sometimes, people who get cochlear implants are not accepted by their deaf peers.

Others who are deaf, as well as some parents of deaf children, look to cochlear implants as a way to integrate with the hearing world. Bill Graham, a trustee at Gallaudet, became deaf when he was in his 20s. He learned ASL and became involved in deaf culture. Ten years later, he decided to get a cochlear implant. He says the implant allowed him to get a new job at a large corporation. "I could deal better with people on the job without needing an interpreter,"[**] he said at a Gallaudet conference on cochlear implants in 1999. He was also pleased to hear his baby daughter's voice.

---

[*] Diana Jean Schemo, "Turmoil at College for Deaf Reflects Larger Debate," *New York Times*, October 21, 2006.

[**] Todd Byrd, "Recipients of Cochlear Implants Tell of Their Experiences." *On The Green*, February 17, 1999. Available online at *http://pr.gallaudet.edu/otg/BackIssues.asp?ID=150*.

Like those in the deaf community, people with serious mental illness have also waged battles for recognition and respect. Stigmatized and hidden away in state hospitals, people with severe mental illness had many obstacles to overcome. In the 1960s, Judi Chamberlain was hospitalized because of depression. A young woman in her early 20s, she found she had no rights as a patient in a state institution. After she got out of the hospital, in the 1970s, Chamberlain founded the Mental Patients Liberation Front, an activist group made up of former patients. She began advocating for changes in the mental health system. Groups like the

Alliance for the Mentally Ill, made up of parents and family members, pushed for better care for their loved ones. Today, most people with mental illnesses live in communities, rather than in hospitals. With the help of medication and support services, more people are encouraged to live up to their potential in their work and personal lives.

DISABILITY CULTURE

The ADA and many other civil rights laws have improved the lives of tens of thousands of people with disabilities. From ATM machines with Braille buttons for people with visual impairments to classrooms in public schools that can accommodate children with learning disabilities, the world has become easier to navigate. "I see progress everyday when I speak with young deaf people. They discuss their plans to become lawyers, or scientists, or accountants, or professors and they in fact succeed in these and many other professions. I assure you that we will continue to work hard to keep the promise of the ADA alive," said Dr. I. King Jordan, former president of Gallaudet. Yet legislative changes are only one step in the quest for disability rights. There is still a ways to go to building a society where people with disabilities are seen as equals. For example, people with disabilities want to stop the slurs and insults often used to describe them. People with mental retardation have had to hear themselves called names like idiot, dummy, retard, or much worse. Even the term *mental retardation* is seen by many to be derogatory. By changing the language, people with disabilitites also change attitudes and gain self-respect.

Rather than hiding their disability, people are celebrating themselves through artistic expression, from painting to blogging, from dancing to writing poetry. The disability culture movement tries to foster pride and a positive self-image and works toward helping society respect diversity. The movement also promotes establishing disability studies in colleges and cataloguing the history of the disabilities movement. Some people call this a "quest for identity," replacing society's negative views with a positive, collective self-image. Rather than just learning to live with a disability, advocates of a disability culture encourage people to develop pride and celebrate their talents. "Yes, we have learned something important about life from being disabled that makes us unique yet affirms our common humanity. We refuse any longer to hide our differences. Rather, we will explore, develop and celebrate our distinctness and offer its lessons to the world,"[33] said Carol Gill, a psychologist who has studied disability culture and is, herself, a polio survivor.

Disability culture activist Simi Linton was on her way from Boston to an antiwar protest in Washington, D.C., in 1971 when she was in a car accident that left both her legs paralyzed and her husband and best friend dead. In her book *My Body Politic: A Memoir*, she writes about how she recovered, earned a doctorate, and found a new life as a disability rights activist. She helped start the Society for Disability Studies, which explores disability from scholarly perspectives. Linton also writes a blog (*http://www.similinton.com/blog/*) about artists, writers, musicians, dancers, and others who explore the idea of disability. Along the way, she learned to live a full life. She even learned to dance with the help of a friend, a quadriplegic who never let his wheelchair get in the way. "Everything I learned about dancing," writes Linton. "I learned from a quadriplegic."[34]

Chicanos Fight
for Their Rights

On a September morning in 1944, Soledad Vidaurri walked with her children and her nieces and nephews to the 17th Street School, a public elementary school in Westminster, California. The Mexican American mother planned to enroll the children for classes. Soledad's two children, Alice and Virginia, who had light complexions, were allowed to sign up, but her brother's children, Sylvia, Gonzalo Jr., and Geronimo Mendez, had darker skin. The administrator told them to go to the school for Mexican American children several blocks away. Vidaurri was so angry that she did not enroll any of the children.

In the 1940s, Mexican Americans, or Chicanos, in California were excluded from "whites only" public parks, restaurants, swimming pools, and schools, though people with lighter skin often escaped discrimination. In the small farming town of Westminster, they worked in the fields and lived in segregated neighborhoods apart from white families. Their children attended the Hoover School, housed in a run-down building next to a cow pasture, while white students attended the more modern 17th Street School, surrounded by lawns and sports fields.

The children's parents, Felicitas and Gonzalo Mendez, emigrated from Mexico when they were young, and they wanted the best education for their children. They wanted their children to attend the 17th Street School. They organized other Chicano parents and wrote to the board of education, demanding the 17th Street School be integrated. The board refused, so the parents hired a civil rights lawyer, who took the case, *Mendez v. Westminster*, to court. In 1946, U.S. District Court judge Paul J. McCormick ruled in favor of the Mendezes, saying that segregation "fosters antagonisms in the children and suggests inferiority among them where none exists."[35] In September 1947, the three Mendez children enrolled at the 17th Street School, and other California cities began integrating their schools. Seven years later, in 1954, the U.S. Supreme Court outlawed segregation in public education facilities in the landmark case *Brown v. Board of Education*. Separate schools for different races could not provide an equal education anywhere in the United States, the justices ruled.

DEEP ROOTS IN AMERICA

The right to attend public schools was one of many battles fought by Chicanos and other Hispanics during the last century. Fed up with second-class citizenship, poor housing, decrepit schools, and blatant discrimination, they took to the streets, the courts, and Congress, and they made significant progress. With persistence, even the migrant farmworkers who toiled in lettuce fields and grape orchards were able to secure better working conditions and basic health and safety rights that most workers take for granted.

Hispanics have deep roots in the United States. Spanish explorers were among the first Europeans to colonize North America. Juan Ponce de León claimed Florida for Spain in 1513. Francisco Vásquez de Coronado rode through the

Southwest in search of the Seven Cities of Cíbola, claiming present-day New Mexico for Spain in 1540. Present-day California also became part of the Spanish Empire. Texas was formerly part of Mexico, but in 1836, Texas revolted; after a six-month war, the Republic of Texas was created. Even then, Mexico did not recognize Texas, but after the United States annexed Texas in 1845, relations between the two countries deteriorated.

In 1846, the United States, determined to expand, declared war on Mexico over land and border issues, specifically whether the Rio Grande or the Nueces River marked the border between Texas and Mexico. When the war ended two years later, Mexico gave up the land that is present-day California, Nevada, and Utah, and parts of Colorado, Arizona, New Mexico, and Wyoming in exchange for a monetary payment. The Mexicans living in the Southwest would eventually become U.S. citizens. In the early twentieth century, thousands more Mexicans fled revolution and poverty to settle in the Southwest and especially California. Then during the Great Depression, Mexicans were not wanted—there was no work for them— and they were forced back to Mexico. World War II boosted the U.S. economy and more workers were needed. From the 1940s to the 1960s, the Bracero Program allowed thousands of Mexican laborers into the United States as guest workers; many stayed on.

On the East Coast, Puerto Rican migration swelled after World War II, as these Caribbean islanders, who are U.S. citizens, sought opportunities in New York and other cities. By the mid-1960s, more than a million Puerto Ricans lived in the United States. Not far from Puerto Rico, Fidel Castro's Communist Revolution in Cuba in 1959 forced thousands of middle-class Cubans to flee to Miami, creating a vibrant Cuban American community in that city.

When Fidel Castro came to power in 1959, many Cubans fled the country after the government seized their property and nationalized industry. Here, several Cubans arrive in Miami, Florida, in January 1961, in the hopes of starting a new life in the United States.

Since the 1960s, immigrants from Central and South America, leaving behind lives of desperate poverty to secure better futures for their families, have expanded the Hispanic population in large cities and small towns alike. By 2000, Hispanics had become the fastest growing minority group in the United States. The 2000 U.S. Census reported 35.2 million Hispanics, or 12.5 percent of the population, up 61 percent since 1990, a number that does not include people without documentation. This diverse group of nationalities, religions, and races has a common aspect—they or their ancestors are native Spanish speakers. As early as the 1900s, Hispanics began organizing to press for equal footing in American society, but it was not until the Chicano movement took root in the 1950s and 1960s that change began to come.

LAND GRANT MOVEMENT

Discontent had been boiling for a long time. Most Chicanos in the 1940s lived in barrios, poor city neighborhoods with substandard housing and without hospitals, banks, and supermarkets, where only Spanish was spoken. Not welcome outside their neighborhoods, they worked at low-paying, dead-end jobs, and their children attended segregated schools. A sense of hopelessness led the young men, especially, to feel angry and resentful. In Los Angeles, some of the young men, calling themselves *pachucos*, wore distinctive haircuts, and clothing known as zoot suits— wide-brimmed hats, long coats, and dangling chains. Violent racial confrontations, known as the Zoot Suit Riots, between young Hispanic and white men during World War II in Los Angeles showed the divide between the ethnic groups. Even First Lady Eleanor Roosevelt felt something had to be done. She wrote in her syndicated weekly newspaper column that the riots indicated a deep-seated racial problem that had to be faced. By the 1950s, people in the barrios felt they had a right to the American dream, too.

A long, bitter land dispute in New Mexico ignited one of the earliest Chicano protests. Historically, colonial Spain, and then Mexico, had given Mexican families land grants, or free land, in present-day New Mexico and Southern Colorado to encourage settlement. Many Mexicans settled there and raised families for generations before the Mexican-American War in 1846. With Mexico's defeat in 1848, the land was now part of the United States. The Treaty of Guadalupe Hidalgo, which ended the war, ensured that the Mexicans living there would eventually become U.S. citizens, and that they could keep their land. The treaty was not honored. The land grants were not upheld, and much of the land was taken by white settlers.

Fed up and angry, land grant activists formed Alianza Federal de Mercedes Reales, or The Federal Alliance of Land Grants, led by an evangelical preacher named Reies López Tijerina, who had grown up picking cotton. In 1967, Tijerina and other activists raided the Tierra Amarilla Courthouse in northern New Mexico to protest the land losses. They attempted to capture the district attorney, a Mexican American who tried to stop the protestors. Shots were fired, and people were injured. U.S. Army tanks were sent in. Tijerina fled, but later turned himself in. While in the Santa Fe jail, he wrote a long letter, similar to the letter Reverend Martin Luther King Jr., wrote in the Birmingham jail. "My only crime is demanding the respect and protection of our property, which has been confiscated illegally by the federal government. . . . We have the evidence to prove our claims to property as well as to the cultural rights of which we have been deprived,"[36] he wrote. Tijerina became known as King Tiger and a hero of the Chicano movement. Dr. King took notice of the New Mexican activists. He sent a telegram to Tijerina, inviting him to join the Poor People's Campaign, a protest held in May 1968 in Washington, D.C.

"NOW THE TRUMPET SOUNDS"

A new pride and identity were born. Although it was once a derogatory slur to insult Mexican Americans, the term *Chicano identity* was adopted by activists to describe a culture and an attitude. The Chicano movement was called "El Movimiento." Chicano boxer, political activist, and poet Rodolfo Corky Gonzales described the movement as the awakening of a "sleeping giant" in his famous 1967 poem, *Yo Soy Joaquín*, or *I Am Joaquín*. Reprinted in Spanish language newspapers throughout the country, the poem became a rallying cry for a new civil rights movement:

> *And now the trumpet sounds,*
> *The music of the people stirs the*
> *Revolution.*
> *Like a sleeping giant it slowly*
> *Rears its head*
> *To the sound of*
> *Tramping feet*
> *Clamoring voices*
> *Mariachi strains*
> *Fiery tequila explosions*
> *The smell of chile verde and*
> *Soft brown eyes of expectation for a*
> *Better life.*

Part of the movement grew from the barrio, where young people who felt marginalized were fueled by anger. At the same time, Chicano lawyers, journalists, politicians, teachers, and social workers added their talents and skills. Organizations such as the Mexican American Legal Defense and Educational Fund (MALDEF) provided leadership. Founded in 1968, MALDEF became an influential civil rights organization, offering community education, advocacy, and legal services. In 1984, MALDEF won the important lawsuit *Edgewood v. Kirby* that challenged Texas's method of financing public schools, which left schools in Hispanic neighborhoods with less funding. As a result of the lawsuit, Texas had to reduce the large funding disparities among school districts.

"WE ARE HUMAN BEINGS"

If a shopper wanted to buy table grapes at a Chicago supermarket in the late 1960s, he or she would probably have to settle for apples or oranges, instead. Throughout the nation, table grapes disappeared from produce sections of supermarkets, and many customers refused to buy the grapes available. Led by Chicano labor organizer César Chávez and the United Farm Workers of America, a national grape boycott was underway to protest the poor treatment of workers in California's vineyards. Vineyard owners had refused to raise wages or allow grape workers to unionize. Strikes and protests had not worked, so the farmworkers chose the boycott as a nonviolent way to pressure the growers. In a letter to the California Grape & Tree Fruit League, asking the growers to bargain with the union, Chávez wrote: "We are men and women who have suffered and endured much and not only because of our abject poverty but because we have been kept poor. The color of our skins, the languages of our cultural and native origins, the lack of formal education, the exclusion from the democratic process . . . all these burdens generation after generation have sought to demoralize us, to break our human spirit."[37] As a result of the five-year boycott, many union contracts were signed.

Chávez knew the life of the migrant farmworker. He was born in 1927 in Yuma, Arizona, where his grandfather, a Mexican immigrant, built a farm and family hacienda. Solidly middle class, Chávez's parents lost the farm and three small businesses in the Great Depression and drought of the 1930s. They packed up and moved to California. Hungry and living in tents in migrant camps, the family went to work as farmworkers. Chávez attended school when he could, but by eighth grade, he was working full time. After two years of service in the U.S. Navy, Chávez returned to California.

Angry at what his family and others had to endure, Chávez joined other labor leaders to press for decent wage and working conditions. He said that the farmworkers were human beings, whose sweat and sacrifice put food on the tables for people throughout the world. Indeed, California's huge agricultural industry relied on Chicanos, Mexicans, Filipinos, and others to pick broccoli, spinach, and peas. The migrant workers followed the crops by season, living in camps without electricity or water. The pay was so poor that children and elderly grandmothers had to do back-breaking labor to help families survive. Job security, health benefits, and pensions were nonexistent.

In 1962, Chávez, along with a young activist named Dolores Huerta and others, helped found a workers association, which became a union, the United Farm Workers of America (UFW). "*Si, se puede*" or "Yes, We can do it" was its motto, and the proud Mexican eagle, its symbol. Dedicated to the nonviolent methods of Mohandas K. Gandhi and Dr. Martin Luther King, Chávez organized strikes, marches, boycotts, and even "*huelga de hambres*" or hunger strikes, to get the message out. After Chávez conducted a 25-day fast in 1968 to reaffirm the farmworkers' commitment to nonviolence, New York senator Robert F. Kennedy flew to Delano, California, to be with him when he ended the fast.

Chávez launched another grape boycott in the 1970s after growers refused to support a collective bargaining law for farmworkers. Under pressure from the workers and the strikes, the 1975 Agricultural Labor Relations Act was enacted and accepted by growers. Chávez also tried to protect farmworkers from the toxic pesticides used in the agricultural fields. "In the old days, miners would carry birds with them to warn against poison gas. Hopefully, the birds would die before the miners. Farm workers are society's canaries,"[38] said Chávez. He conducted another hunger strike in 1988, fasting for 36 days to bring attention

In 1968, labor leader César Chávez conducted a 25-day hunger strike to affirm his dedication to the farmworkers' movement and their nonviolent forms of protest. Here, Chávez is pictured with New York senator Robert F. Kennedy, who offers support to Chávez at the end of his fast.

to the damaging effects pesticides have on farmworkers. Chávez died in 1993 at the age of 66, a crusader for social justice. More than 50,000 people, many carrying red and black UFW flags, gathered in Delano for his funeral. They marched with his coffin through the streets. One of the mourners was Baldemar Velasquez, a farmworker organizer from Ohio. "Cesar opened up the world of possibility for us. He showed us we could win in our own struggle,"[39] said Velasquez. Today, streets and parks bear his name, and his birthday is celebrated as a state holiday in California and other states.

CHICANO POWER!

The farmworkers movement, in the midst of the tumultuous 1960s, energized Hispanics, who had for decades been

A EULOGY FOR RUFINO CONTRERAS

On February 10, 1979, Rufino Contreras, a striking UFW lettuce cutter, was shot by three lettuce company foremen when he and several other strikers tried to walk onto a lettuce field to talk to workers who had been brought in to take their place. Several days later, standing on a flatbed truck in front of thousands of farmworkers, César Chávez delivered Contreras's eulogy at his open air funeral in Calexico, California. In the following excerpt, Chávez speaks of the sacrifice Contreras made for his fellow farmworkers through his hard work and sacrifice:

Capitol and labor together produce the fruit of the land. But what really counts is labor: the human beings, who torture their bodies, sacrifice their youth and numb their spirits to produce this great agricultural wealth? A wealth so vast that it feeds all of America and much of the world. And yet the men, women and children who are the flesh and blood of this production often do not have enough to feed themselves.

But we are here today to say that true wealth is not measured in money or status or power. It is measured in the legacy that we leave behind for those we love and those we inspire. In that sense, Rufino is not dead. Wherever farm workers organize, stand up for their rights and strike for justice, Rufino Contreras is with them. Rufino lives among us. It is those who have killed him and those who have conspired to kill him that has died; because the love, the compassion, the light in their hearts have been stilled.[*]

[*] César Chávez. "Eulogy for Rufino Contreras." United Farm Workers of America. Available online at *http://www.ufw.org/_page.php?menu=research&inc=history/11.html*.

pushed to society's edges. Young Chicano students began to demand respect and recognition. Paula Crisostomo was a 17-year-old high school senior at Lincoln High School in East Los Angeles in 1968. Though she was bound for college,

Crisostomo was upset at the poor education provided to Mexican American students. Banned from speaking Spanish in the classroom, the boys were pushed toward studying auto mechanics and the girls toward pursuing secretarial work or marriage, rather than college. Crisostomo and other students decided to take action.

Approximately 20,000 Hispanic students in Los Angeles walked out of school in March 1968 to demand more Chicano teachers, Mexican history and culture classes, better facilities, and college prep courses. At the time, Senator Robert Kennedy met with student leaders to offer support. Kennedy was running for president, but a few months later, on June 5, he was assassinated. During the walkout, students carried "Viva La Raza" signs, and shouted "Chicano Power!" as they took to the streets. Their parents staged sit-in protests at the district attorney's office. Thirteen leaders were arrested. "It's not about having power over the other people. It's not about separating yourselves. It was about reclaiming our own human dignity, reclaiming our own human power,"[40] recalled Moctesuma Esparza who was arrested during the protests. He later helped produce the 2007 HBO film *Walkout*, which recaptured the events. Some of the students' demands were met, and progress was made.

Soon afterward, in the Chicano neighborhood of East Los Angeles, a group of young men formed the Brown Berets, a paramilitary organization similar to the Black Panthers. The Brown Berets lasted about five years, staging civil rights and antiwar protests. They joined other antiwar activists to form the National Chicano Moratorium Committee against the Vietnam War. On August 29, 1970, the group organized a massive march in East Los Angeles to protest the disproportionately high numbers of Chicano soldiers killed in Vietnam. Approximately 30,000 people joined the protest, which soon became violent. Looters broke into stores, and buildings were sent on fire.

A popular Chicano journalist named Rubén Salazar was killed by a tear gas canister thrown into the Silver Dollar Café by a sheriff's deputy. One of the few Chicano journalists in the mainstream media at the time, he was an editor for a local TV station and wrote hundreds of articles on the Chicano community for the *Los Angeles Times*. His death, a great loss to Chicanos, sparked outrage and investigations, but no charges were filed against the deputy. "He was the only journalist in L.A. with real influence who would come to a press conference in the barrio,"[41] said one activist after his death.

A NEW POLITICAL PARTY

A Mexican American, Ezequiel de Baca was elected governor of New Mexico in 1918, and other Hispanics won political office in the early twentieth century, but not many. Edward R. Roybal was one of very few Hispanic politicians by the 1960s. By organizing and getting out the vote in Chicano neighborhoods, Roybal was able to win a seat in the Los Angeles city council from 1949 to 1962. He went on to the U.S. House of Representatives in 1962, where he supported bilingual education and fought for fair housing laws, rights for the elderly, and civil rights for immigrants until his retirement 30 years later. Still, the more militant Chicano activists felt that neither the Republicans nor Democrats represented their interests. For the most part, they felt they had no voice in the political process.

In January 1970, Chicanos in Crystal City, Texas, began a movement to establish a third political party, La Raza Unida, or "The Race United Party." Organizers in California, New Mexico, and Colorado began La Raza Unida chapters to work on local issues. The party fielded candidates in local school committee and city council elections and conducted write-in campaigns that often split results. In 1972, La Raza members met in El Paso, Texas, and organized a party platform, stating their goals, including bilingual education, services to Chicano neighborhoods, migrant children education, national health insurance, and the election of Mexican American judges. They also elected a chairman, José Angel Gutiérrez. "Without funds, without a staff, without real political experience, about 500 activist Mexican Americans formed a new political party formally here shortly before dawn today,"[42] wrote a *New York Times* reporter in attendance.

During the following decades, more Hispanics would win office in local and state elections, but only gradually. When Antonio Villaraigosa, a Chicano, was elected mayor of Los Angeles in 2005, he became the first Hispanic since the nineteenth century to lead the city, despite a 46 percent Hispanic population. Nationally, voting rates among Hispanics lag behind blacks and whites. In the 2004 November elections, Hispanics cast 6 percent of the vote, even though they comprise more than 12 percent of the population, according to the Pew Hispanic Center, a nonpartisan research center. Just 58 percent of eligible voters are registered, compared to 75 percent of whites and 69 percent of blacks.

MAMBO MUSIC AND MANGO STREET

César Chávez encouraged artists to make posters for his labor campaigns, helping to spark a movement known as Chicano Art. Posters, street murals, and other public art championed themes such as justice, freedom, and Chicano culture. In 1970, a young Chicana artist named Judith F. Baca gathered her paint buckets and enlisted young people from rival Chicano gangs in Los Angeles to help her paint *"Mí*

Abuelita" or "My Grandmother" in a local park. The giant painting of a grandmother, the central figure in Mexican families, filled the walls of a concrete bandstand. "Perhaps it was the abundance of concrete, or the year-round painting season, or the city full of Mexican workers that made Los Angeles the place where murals began to be a predominant art form. Or perhaps it was because an entire population— the majority of the city—had been 'disappeared' in textbooks, in the media, in cultural markers of place, and needed to find a way to reclaim a city of Mexican and indigenous roots,"[43] said Baca in a PBS interview.

In 1976, Baca, with hundreds of young volunteers, as well as historians and educators, began to paint *The Great Wall of Los Angeles*. The giant mural depicts California history through its ethnic groups, and runs a half-mile along the Tujunga Flood Control Channel in the San Fernando Valley. The project took five summers to complete, and it is now being restored. Baca became the director of a public mural program for the City of Los Angeles, and more murals were painted in the barrios. Murals and other public art are a way to celebrate Chicano pride and identity.

SALSA

Starting with salsa, Latin music also entered the cultural mainstream, influencing American pop music and drawing large audiences. Salsa is an up-tempo dance music with roots in Afro-Cuban music. The music was popularized by musicians such as Tito Puente, Celia Cruz, and Ruben Blades, a Panamanian singer and actor who combined salsa with African rhythms, jazz, rock, and blues. Salsa was only the beginning, as talented Hispanic singers and musicians blended many genres that caught on with the listening public. In 1999, the Puerto Rican singer Ricky Martin, who began his career with Spanish-language albums, scored a hit with his song "Livin' La Vida Loca." Other musicians such as Jennifer Lopez, Enrique Iglesias, and Marc Anthony have helped make Latin-influenced music more popular. Shakira, a Colombian performer, sings in English and Spanish; she has won both Grammys and Latin Grammys for her many number one songs and albums.

In American literature, Hispanic writers have created a new genre. They offer strong, engaging looks at both the immigrant experience and lives left behind in Cuba, Mexico, and South America. Oscar Hijuelos was the first Hispanic to win the Pulitzer Prize for fiction for his 1989 novel, *The Mambo Kings Play Songs of Love*. His parents were Cuban but he was born in New York City in 1951. His book is about two Cuban musicians who immigrate to New York and play mambo music. Sandra Cisneros wrote about the lives of urban Mexican Americans in her 1988 young-adult novel, *The House on Mango Street*. Esmerelda, a Mexican American girl, like Cisneros, grows up in working-class Chicago, and worries that her schoolmates don't know how to say her name. "All brown all around, we are safe. But watch us drive into a neighborhood of another color and our knees go shakity-shake and our car windows get rolled up tight and our eyes look straight. Yeah. That is how it goes and goes,"[44] says Esmerelda.

BILINGUAL EDUCATION

For Hispanic children who could not speak or read English, school posed serious challenges in the 1960s. No special classes were offered to help them learn English. In some states, schools forbid the use of other languages, and students got in trouble if they spoke Spanish. Their parents who spoke only Spanish were unable to help at home. A senator from Texas, Ralph Yarborough, was concerned that so many Hispanic students were failing in public schools. A liberal in a conservative state, Yarborough pushed forward legislation to mandate better native-language instruction. Congress passed the Bilingual Education Act of 1968, which provided federal funding for public schools and led the way for states to start programs for students whose native language was not English—not just Spanish, but Chinese, Russian, and other languages.

Bilingual classes teach students in both English and their native language, while encouraging them to learn English. Bilingual education was controversial from the start. Not everyone agreed that students should be taught, even partly, in their native language. Nor did some people want public money spent on classes in other languages. Lawsuits were filed after many states dragged their feet. In 1974, the Supreme Court ruled in *Lau v. Nichols* that schools in California had to provide extra help to those students who had limited English proficiency; otherwise, they violated the students' civil rights. In 2000, voters in Arizona passed a proposition banning bilingual education; the state is now under court order to find alternative ways to educate students who need to learn English. Other states have also eliminated bilingual classes and focus instead on English emersion and other techniques.

LEGACY OF "EL MOVIMIENTO"

More than six decades after the Mendez children were allowed to attend public school, Hispanics are an integral part of American society, adding to the vibrancy of contemporary life. Hispanic culture is evident in the food we eat, from salsa to burritos, and the music we sing. From astronauts to baseball players, from entertainers to doctors and lawyers, along with ordinary working families, they have made significant contributions to society. Yet despite innumerable success stories, the sense of injustice

During the spring of 2006, thousands of Hispanics gathered throughout the United States to demand more rights for undocumented immigrants. Here, Marta Sanchez and her son Angel Jr. (in red) demonstrate during an immigration rally in Porterville, California, on May 1 of that year, a day when more than 500,000 undocumented immigrants took to the streets in the state.

and inequality that inspired the Chicano movement in the 1960s still lingers. Many families, trapped by language barriers, lack of education, and uncertain immigration status, still struggle. Nearly 22 percent of Hispanics live in poverty, and 32 percent of Hispanics—and one in five of Hispanic children—do not have health insurance, according to a 2004 U.S. Census Bureau report. Hispanics who are illegal immigrants must hold jobs, go to school, and raise families, while living in constant uncertainty without proper documentation.

During the spring of 2006, hundreds of thousands of Hispanics gathered in protests throughout the country to demand more rights for undocumented immigrants, while Congress debated stricter controls on illegal immigration. In Atlanta, Georgia, a young mother and her children wore T-shirts that read "We are not criminals." In Washington, D.C., protestors waved flags that said "We are America" and chanted "Si, Se Puede," an echo of César Chávez's motto. "The sleeping giant is awake—wide awake—and we're paying close attention,"[45] said organizer Jaime Contreras, president of the National Capital Immigration Coalition, in a CNN interview. The protestors seemed to echo Rodolfo Corky Gonzales's words in his famous poem, *Yo Soy Joaquin*, written nearly 50 years earlier, *"The odds are great / But my spirit is strong."*

5

America's Seniors Speak Out

In June 2006, a group of senior citizens wearing handcuffs gathered in the State House rotunda in Providence, Rhode Island. They had come together to convince state legislators to spend more public funds on home and community care for the elderly, rather than nursing homes. The handcuffs symbolized the lack of choice for frail seniors. Most seniors would prefer to live at home with support services than to move to a nursing home. Rhode Island spends 90 percent of its long-term care funds on nursing homes, and only 10 percent for home and community care. "I'm not a child. I don't want anybody to treat me as a child. I want to be able to choose,"[46] said Irene Santos, president of the Rhode Island chapter of the Gray Panthers, a senior activist organization.

Ever since the 1960s, seniors like Irene Santos have been marching to the state house, knocking on the doors of Congress, and going to the ballot box, trying to improve the lives of elderly Americans. Elder advocates have lobbied for new laws to prevent elder abuse, worked to secure safer care in nursing homes, and battled age discrimination in the workplace. Many landmark federal programs for seniors were established, including Medicare, the federal health insurance program for the elderly, because senior advocates pushed hard. Along the way, seniors gained self-respect and the respect of others. People are listening to their voices. The senior vote is now crucial to politicians looking to win elections. Unlike other minority or special-interest groups, the elderly is an identity group that every person will join as they grow older. Early on, the federal government recognized that what was good for a senior was good for the country.

"A DECENT AND DIGNIFIED SUBSISTENCE"

Before the 1930s, the elderly had only themselves, their families, and their neighbors to rely on as they got older. Men and women unable to live independently often wound up in poorhouses, local institutions set up by county governments to house and feed the most vulnerable citizens of all ages. By the early twentieth century, poorhouses were like old age homes, with mostly elderly tenants, but the situation worsened after the stock market crashed in 1929. The country fell into the Great Depression, an economic crisis that resulted in widespread job loss that crippled families and communities. The depression was particularly hard on the nation's elderly. The traditional American belief in self-sufficiency and independence was not working. Millions of older citizens slipped into poverty and hunger.

Thousands of handwritten letters arrived at the White House, personally addressed to President Franklin D. Roosevelt. Many writers requested help for impoverished elderly relatives. "I write to ask your assistance in securing an old age pension for my mother. . . . She is helpless, suffering from sugar diabetes, which has affected her mind. . . . She is out of funds completely," wrote Mrs. M. A. Zoller of Beaumont, Texas. The president's office promptly responded: "My dear Mrs. Zoller . . . We are in favor of Old Age Pensions and are glad to have your letter."[47] Those were not just hollow words from the president. Pushed by a groundswell of need, the Roosevelt administration established programs from 1933 to 1937 to provide economic relief, recovery, and reform. These and other social programs were collectively known as the New Deal.

SOCIAL SECURITY

On August 14, 1935, Roosevelt signed the landmark legislation establishing the Social Security system. For the first time, a federal safety net was set up for the most vulnerable citizens—the disabled, widows and children, and elderly. "We can never insure one hundred percent of the population against one hundred percent of the hazards and vicissitudes of life, but we have tried to frame a law which will give some measure of protection to the average citizen and to his family against the loss of a job and against poverty-ridden old age,"[48] stated Roosevelt on signing the historic bill. The Social Security system signaled a willingness by American society to share responsibility for older people.

With Social Security, seniors gained the right to a monthly stipend to help pay for basic necessities. Workers invest money in the Social Security system every month through automatic payroll taxes deducted from their paychecks. In return, after they retire, they receive monthly benefits. Spouses and dependents also benefit from this support. Even so, the monthly payment was not enough to sustain most people. They needed savings, pensions, and other support. In addition, over several generations, the Social Security system would become dangerously insecure as fewer workers were investing money in a system that had to pay for an increasing number of retirees.

AN ARMY OF OLDER AMERICANS

With the help of Social Security checks, many seniors were able to retire more comfortably, giving them more leisure

"HUMANE AND PRACTICAL"

President Franklin D. Roosevelt had a right-hand woman who helped draft the New Deal programs. Economist and social worker Frances Perkins was Roosevelt's secretary of labor from 1933 to 1945. Born in Boston and educated at Mount Holyoke College, Perkins witnessed the tragic fire in the Triangle Shirtwaist Factory in Manhattan in 1911. She watched young workers, trapped in a building with locked doors and no fire escapes, jump out the window to their deaths. Horrified at what she had seen, Perkins became an advocate for better protections for workers. When the plight of the nation's vulnerable elderly landed on her desk in the Labor Department, she was just as concerned. In a National Radio Address on February 25, 1935, Perkins said this:

> I come now to the other major phase of our program. The plan for providing against need and dependency in old age is divided into three separate and distinct parts. We advocate, first, free Federally-aided pensions for those now old and in need; second, a system of compulsory contributory old-age insurance for workers in the lower income brackets, and third, a voluntary system of low-

time. Retirees saw that they had a higher stake in government because they needed to protect the Social Security system. More seniors became politically involved, and politicians began to listen. "Social Security enabled this group to become the political powerhouse that they are today. It gave seniors resources—free time and money—because it enabled them to retire, with a pension. Social Security also had the effect of increasing their interest in politics, because they get such a large share of income from the government," said Andrea Louise Campbell, a Harvard professor who studies the elderly and politics. "Social Security takes this otherwise disparate group and lends them a new political identity, creating a group that is ripe for political mobilization by interest groups and political parties."[49]

cost annuities purchasable by those who do not come under the compulsory system.

Enlightened opinion has long since discarded the old poor-house method of caring for the indigent aged, and 28 States already have old-age pension laws. Due to financial difficulties, many of these laws are now far less effective than they were intended to be. Public sentiment in this country is strongly in favor of providing these old people with a decent and dignified subsistence in their declining years. Exploiting that very creditable sentiment, impossible, hare-brained schemes for providing for the aged have sprung into existence and attracted misguided supporters. But the administration is confident that its plan for meeting the situation is both humane and practical and will receive the enthusiastic support of the people.*

* Frances Perkins, "Social Insurance for U.S." Social Security History, Social Security Online. Available online at *http://www.ssa.gov/history/perkinsradio.html*.

Social Security is a safety net, but the monthly checks could not sustain most seniors. Even before the depression, senior advocates pushed for worker pensions. Pensions are a regular income given to an employee after retirement. Pensions are paid by employers, the government, or unions. By the late 1940s, a retired California schoolteacher who was concerned about the economic straits of retired teachers began to push for broader benefits for retirees. In 1947, Ethel Percy Andrus, an educator who was the first female high school principal in California, founded the National Retired Teachers Association. She saw that retired teachers lived on small pensions and did not have health insurance. Like many older people, retired teachers had to rely on savings that were not sufficient. The association advocated for health benefits and pension protections for its members. Andrus wrote to dozens of insurance companies, requesting health insurance for retired teachers. Finally, in 1956, an insurance company agreed to issue policies.

As time went on, Andrus recognized that retired teachers were not the only seniors who needed more support. In 1958, she expanded her organization to become the American Association of Retired Persons (AARP). The AARP, a nonprofit and nonpartisan organization, was eventually opened to anyone older than the age of 50. Today, the AARP, often referred to as "an army of older Americans," is a powerful organization with more than 35 million dues-paying members, and its spoon is in many pots. Virtually all Americans nearing their fiftieth birthday receive unsolicited requests to join the AARP—it is almost like a rite of passage into senior citizenship. Along with offering health and life insurance policies, an array of publications, and additional information sources, the AARP is a powerful lobbying force in Washington, D.C., taking on issues from healthcare to employment.

Not everyone is a fan of the AARP. The organization is nonpartisan, or not attached to any political party, but critics have charged that the AARP's lobbying efforts have veered toward so-called liberal causes, not always reflecting its diverse membership. In general, the AARP has sided with policies supported by the Democrats, but in 2003 the AARP supported the Republican plan to add a prescription drug benefit to Medicare. The plan was controversial. Democrats felt it would weaken Medicare because it does not require drug companies to keep prices down. Many AARP members did not agree with the plan and quit the organization. William D. Novelli, chief executive of AARP at the time, stood by the organization's decision, saying that the plan was needed to help the system take on the

Founded in 1958 by Ethel Percy Andrus, the American Association of Retired Persons (AARP) is dedicated to enhancing the quality of life for people age 50 and above. The AARP is the nation's largest organization representing senior citizens and is one of the largest lobbying groups in the United States. Here, AARP members rally in support of improved long-term care services at the Virginia state capitol in Richmond on January 24, 2007.

large numbers of people nearing retirement. "We have some repair work to do with the Medicare legislation and members' views of it (but) we did the right thing. The boomers are coming, and the country is not ready,"[50] said Novelli. In 2003, the Medicare Prescription Drug Law was signed into law, creating a voluntary drug benefit plan known as Part D of Medicare. Beginning in 2006, seniors signed up with private health insurance companies to get coverage for prescription drugs. The procedure was confusing and controversial. Seniors had to do a lot of research to find the best plans; the costs varied from plan to plan, but as months passed, the general consensus was that the program was working fairly well.

OLDER AMERICANS ACT AND MEDICARE

Starting in the 1950s, elder advocates, as well as politicians, began talking about setting a national agenda for elder issues. No federal agency was in place to oversee the needs of the elderly or to act as a clearinghouse for information and services. In 1959, a Senate subcommittee held hearings throughout the country, and seniors stood up and told their stories. In 1961, people gathered to discuss issues from healthcare to nursing homes at the first White House Conference on Aging. From this important conference, which has reconvened every 10 years since then, emerged a new national determination to confront elder issues in a more organized way.

Thanks to the tireless efforts of senior advocates, such as the AARP and the National Council of Senior Citizens, on July 14, 1965, President Lyndon B. Johnson signed the Older Americans Act (OAA). This important legislation was part of Johnson's larger plan to help low-income people, known as the War on Poverty. The OAA addressed the needs of seniors on several fronts. The Administration on Aging was established as a federal agency within the U.S. Department of Health and Human Services. The agency provides grants to states for local services to the elderly in their own communities. The OAA was amended during the decades that followed to add nutrition programs for homebound elderly, health promotion and disease prevention, and in-home services for frail elderly, among other programs, establishing crucial lifelines for seniors throughout the country.

Providing better healthcare for the elderly was a major goal of both legislators and advocates, but the question was how to do it. The AARP and several other senior organizations joined labor unions to push for federal health insurance for the elderly and the poor. The senior advocates and union workers leading the drive had many issues in common, and they built up a strong front. They were facing an even stronger coalition: the medical establishment, large corporations, and others who felt that an insurance program would be too expensive. The American Medical Association stated that publicly provided medical care for the elderly would be "dangerous to the principles underlying our American system of medical care," wrote Lawrence A. Powell and his coauthors in their book *The Senior Rights Movement*. Powell wrote that the issue became a battle between "the have's and the have nots."[51]

In the end, most people agreed that the United States needed a health safety net for society's most vulnerable citizens. In 1965, President Johnson signed into law amendments to the Social Security Act that created Medicare and Medicaid, the federal health insurance programs for people who cannot afford to pay for medical care. Medicaid provides healthcare to people who meet certain income and disability guidelines, while Medicare is the federal health insurance program for people older than the age of 65. At the signing ceremony, President Johnson said:

> No longer will older Americans be denied the healing miracle of modern medicine. No longer will illness crush and destroy the savings that they have so carefully put away over a lifetime so that they might enjoy dignity in their later years. No longer will young families see their own incomes, and their own hopes, eaten away simply because they are carrying out their deep moral obligations to their parents, and to their uncles, and their aunts.[52]

Johnson signed the historic law at the Harry S. Truman Presidential Library in Independence, Missouri, where he was accompanied by the former president. Truman had tried unsuccessfully to establish health insurance for the elderly 20 years earlier. He was the first person to sign up for Medicare. Today, Medicare helps provide medical and health services to approximately 43 million older Americans. Medicare helps pay for healthcare, but it does not cover all the costs. Recipients are required to pay monthly premiums for certain services, including prescription drug coverage.

"WELL-AIMED SLINGSHOTS CAN TOPPLE GIANTS"

Many individuals have made a difference in the fight for senior rights. One of the most well-known is Maggie Kuhn, a feisty and energetic social activist, born in 1905. Kuhn had worked for the Presbyterian Church in Philadelphia for many years, but when she turned 65 years old, she was forced to retire. Angry that she could no longer work, Kuhn was dismayed to be a victim of ageism, the negative attitude toward older people shown by discrimination and prejudice. "In the first month after I was ordered to retire, I felt dazed and suspended. I was hurt and then, as time passed, outraged. . . . Something clicked in my mind. I saw that my problem was not mine alone . . . something was fundamentally wrong with a system that had no use for people like me,"[53] she wrote in her autobiography. Kuhn and her friends founded the Gray Panthers, modeling their name after the Black Panthers, the radical African American civil rights organization. Not restricted to older people, the Gray Panthers attracted college and high school students, too. "Age and Youth in Action," was their motto, and they took on many social issues from nuclear disarmament to nursing homes.

The Gray Panthers believe that aging was just one part of a person's life, and that it can be a wonderful time of growth and activity. They marched in rallies, testified before Congress, and spoke out against issues like ageism and mandatory retirement, and to improve retirement programs such as pension systems. "Ageism is just as pervasive in our society as sexism,"[54] Kuhn said at a church conference in 1972. Believing that many social issues were interrelated, the Gray Panthers joined other groups to protest the Vietnam War, nuclear proliferation, and other hot-button controversies of the era. Today, Gray Panther groups are still providing a

After being forced to retire from her job with the Presbyterian Church when she turned 65, Maggie Kuhn founded the Gray Panthers to protect the rights of senior citizens. Kuhn is pictured here during the White House's third Conference on Aging in December 1981.

platform for seniors in cities throughout the country. "Speak your mind even if your voice shakes for well-aimed slingshots can topple giants," was one of Kuhn's favorite phrases.

Having been forced to retire because of her age, Kuhn worked tirelessly to keep older Americans in the workforce. By the 1960s, many employers, including the federal government, instituted mandatory retirement rules that required workers to retire when they reached a certain age. This allowed younger employees to be hired but put a burden on older workers who wanted or needed to keep their jobs. Kuhn and the Gray Panthers called mandatory retirement "age discrimination" and considered it a civil rights issue. The Gray Panthers, the AARP, and other senior rights organizations pushed for laws to protect older workers from mandatory retirement and other job discrimination. They argued that ending mandatory retirement would also take pressure off the Social Security system. If older workers continued working for a few more years, they would receive Social Security checks later in life, and for a shorter amount of time. Congress listened to their arguments.

AGE DISCRIMINATION IS OUTLAWED

In 1967, Congress passed legislation that marked a major step toward protecting the jobs of older workers. The Age Discrimination in Employment Act of 1967, known as the ADEA, protects workers who are 40 years of age or older from employment discrimination based on age. This law, which has been amended since then, applies to both employees and people applying for jobs. Older workers cannot be discriminated against when it comes to job assignments, benefits, training, layoffs, or any other activities in the workplace. The law also prohibits mandatory retirement by making it unlawful to discharge any employee because of age. Mandatory retirement age rules are permitted in certain occupations that involve public safety, such as police, firefighters, federal law enforcement officers, air traffic controllers, and commercial airline pilots.

The issue is ongoing. In February 2007, the Federal Aviation Administration (FAA) announced a new proposal to change the mandatory retirement age for airline pilots from 60 to 65. "We are heartened to see such a positive change in the attitude of the FAA toward older pilots. Job retention should be grounded in demonstrated competence—not age," said Mary Martin, chairman of The Seniors Coalition, an advocacy group, in a press release. "We have been working hard for this because we believe that age discrimination is inherently wrong. And we will continue to press the FAA on this proposal until it becomes their official practice."[55]

The passage of civil rights laws for seniors was only a first step. Like other identity groups, seniors have to be vigilant to make sure the laws are enforced. For example, employers do not always adhere to the laws against age discrimination in the workplace set out by the ADEA. Workers who believe they are discriminated against can choose to file a complaint with the U.S. Equal Employment and Opportunity Commission (EEOC), a federal agency. Each year, thousands of age-related complaints are filed. In the fiscal year 2006, the EEOC received 13,569 charges of age discrimination and resolved more than 14,000 age discrimination cases. Individuals recovered $51.5 million in benefits that year.

NURSING HOME REFORM

One of the most difficult challenges for the senior movement has been to ensure the health and safety of the most feeble elderly, many of whom live in nursing homes. In 1958, a team of investigators went on a series of surprise night raids of nursing homes in New York City. What they found was shocking: frail elderly were starving and uncared for, even though the nursing home operators were being paid top rates with public funds. States began licensing nursing homes in the 1950s, but conditions varied widely, and there was little oversight and few standards of care. Under pressure from senior activists, federal nursing home regulations were put in place with the start of Medicare and Medicaid in 1965. Nursing homes receiving these federal funds had to follow a set of standard health and safety and care guidelines or lose the money. In 1967, Congress passed the first set of nursing home standards, but activists knew they had to get out into the communities in order to make sure that the standards were upheld. After all, many of the nursing home residents could not speak for themselves.

In 1975, a group of senior activists attended a nursing home industry conference in Washington, D.C. Many of them had personal experience with family members in nursing homes. They spoke of their concerns about the poor care in nursing homes and what needed to be done to improve conditions for the patients. One of the activists, Elma Holder, a member of the Gray Panthers, decided to found a new organization, the National Citizens' Coalition for Nursing Home Reform (NCCNHR), to give a voice to families and patients in nursing homes. Two years later, Holder published a citizens' guide for organizing and achieving nursing home reform in communities. She encouraged people to visit nursing homes and take action on the local level.

In 1986, Holder organized the Campaign for Quality Care, a group of more than 100 organizations that worked together to push for nursing home reform at the federal level. The group provided proposals for the Omnibus Budget Reconciliation Act of 1987, a major piece of legislation that included an important nursing home reform package. For the first time, the quality of care in nursing homes was a priority, and a patient's "bill of rights" for residents was included. Nursing homes had to provide care in a way that would maintain or enhance the quality of life for every resident. Reduction in the use of tranquilizers and physical restraints was required, as well as better training for staff. This historic legislation is known as the Nursing Home Reform Act. The battle was not over, and two decades later, nursing home advocates still face many of the same issues, from inadequate staffing to poor care in some facilities, but thanks to Holden and other activists, a solid start had been made toward recognizing the rights of the frailest citizens.

THE SENIOR VOTE

A few weeks before the mayoral election in November 2005, New York City Mayor Michael Bloomberg attended ceremonies for the opening of a new senior center in Chinatown. Bloomberg was running for his second term, and even though attending the event was not part of his campaign, he knew his presence would not hurt. The senior center, proposed for the basement of an opulent co-op apartment building, had been the focus of a long battle between local seniors and the co-op residents, who worried about noise, food smells, and other disruptions in the building. The seniors had filed lawsuits and rallied on the sidewalk to convince the co-op board to allow the senior center. Finally, the center opened. In his address to the crowd, Bloomberg said a few words in Chinese. "*Ni ja hao*," he said, meaning "everybody is good." "It's an honor to be on board for these seniors who have done so much for this city," he said. The director of the senior center, Po Ling Ng, thanked Bloomberg for being there, and then urged all the seniors in the room to give him their vote.[56]

Like most politicians, Bloomberg, who went on to win the election, knows the value of reaching out to seniors.

Like all savvy politicians, New York mayor Michael Bloomberg knows the importance of reaching out to senior citizens: voters older than the age of 65 are the largest voting block in the country. Here, Bloomberg dances with 100-year-old Bertha Berman during a visit to Brooklyn's Senior League of Flatbush in September 2003.

Stops at senior centers and bingo halls are an important part of any political campaign. Voters older than the age of 65 are the largest voting block in the country. Thus, politicians campaign hard for the "senior vote." In 2004, 79 percent of people ages 65 to 74 years old were registered to vote, and 73 percent actually voted. Younger people vote less often: Only 58 percent of people ages 18 to 24 were registered to vote in 2004, and 47 percent of them went to the polls, according to the U.S. Census Bureau. Politicians on the campaign trail rarely forget to stop at a local senior center to rally the vote. "You win elections with turnout, and seniors are renowned for their turnout," commented Susan MacManus in the *AARP*

Bulletin in 2004. MacManus is a professor of political science at the University of South Florida and the author of the book *Targeting Senior Voters: Campaign Outreach to Elders and Others with Special Needs*. "While a lot of people are projecting an increase in younger voter turnout, it's the senior voters who are the tried and true and can be counted on to show up and cast their ballots,"[57] she wrote.

Still, unlike other identity groups, older voters do not always agree at the polls. Seniors include voters of all races, religions, and political viewpoints. Because they are so diverse—after all, the only thing they may have in common is their age—they cannot be counted on to vote for one candidate or issue. When an issue affects them, such as Social Security or Medicare funding, they will be listening closely to a politician's stance. During the 2000 presidential election, issues like Social Security, long-term care, and Medicare were at the top of the agenda for the two candidates, Vice President Al Gore and then-Texas governor George W. Bush, who went on to win the election. Included among the large number of senior voters were the first wave of baby boomers, then just entering retirement. The baby boomers, or the post–World War II generation born between 1946 and 1964, were becoming increasingly concerned about elder issues. Gore and Bush had different views on the issues, and each tried to convince voters that he was right.

The concerns of the elderly will become increasingly important as the population of older Americans grows rapidly in coming years. By 2030, one in five Americans, or about 72 million people, will be 65 years old or older, according to the National Institutes of Health. The country needs to be sure this large population will be secure. The future of Social Security has become a critical issue for the nation's elderly. As the senior population grows in number, and the younger workforce shrinks, the system is expected to become underfunded and may not be able to pay out the retirement benefits it has promised. In 1950, 16.5 workers paid taxes for every retiree who received benefits; but by 2005, 3.3 workers were paying taxes for each retiree, according to the Social Security Administration. This imbalanced ratio between worker and retiree is expected to worsen during the coming decades. By 2017, the federal government will pay out more benefits than it collects from workers' payroll taxes. By 2041, the system may be bankrupt, according to White House estimates in 2006.

The dilemma facing the United States is whether to keep the Social Security system as it is, or to come up with a better way to keep it solvent. Debates over how to save the Social Security system from financial disaster have been intense, but any reform is extremely controversial. Social Security is considered a bedrock of American society, and many people are reluctant to make changes, fearing more financial risks for seniors. In 2005, the AARP and other senior groups lobbied against the Bush administration's proposal to invest Social Security taxes in private investment accounts, and the plan was shelved, at least temporarily. No doubt, seniors will share their opinions on this issue for years to come. "It will be very difficult to do anything without AARP's support," said Senator Charles E. Grassley, who is chairman of the Senate Finance Committee, in an interview with the *Washington Post.* "And it would be a heck of a lot easier if they came along."[58]

6

Gays in the United States

In the early morning hours of Saturday, June 28, 1969, plain clothes policemen stormed the Stonewall Inn, a popular gay bar in Greenwich Village. The New York City police had raided gay bars before, but this time the customers who had been pushed onto the streets began a protest. They felt unfairly singled out because they were gay. Men threw bricks, garbage, and even a parking meter at the police, who searched the bar on suspicion of liquor license violations. For three nights afterward, the street was filled with angry protestors who posted handwritten signs that read "Support gay power" and "Legalize gay bars" on the boarded-up Stonewall Inn.[59]

The Stonewall Inn riots marked the unofficial start of the gay liberation movement, later known as the gay rights movement, an effort by homosexuals to come out of the closet and into mainstream American society. Until the 1960s, gays and lesbians lived mostly in secrecy, hiding their identities from families, employers, landlords, and even doctors and friends. Only in large cities like New York and San Francisco did gays feel freer to express their individuality. In those cities, they created a strong subculture in the 1920s and 1930s. In most of the United States, though, they were shunned. Homosexuality was viewed as unnatural, immoral, psychologically aberrant, and even criminal. Homophobia, or hatred and fear of gays and lesbians, was entrenched in society.

After World War II, the rise of the cold war, which divided the world into Communist and non-Communist nations, contributed to a sense of national anxiety. In this climate of fear, homosexuals were considered to be enemies that might undermine the morality of the nation, not unlike people suspected of being Communists. The fact that they had to live in secret and hide their identities could even pose a national security threat, according to some people. In 1953, President Dwight Eisenhower signed Executive Order 10450, banning homosexuals from federal jobs. Even the medical profession did not accept them: The American Psychiatric Association listed homosexuality as a mental disorder.

Gay men and lesbians knew that being honest about their sexual orientation could lead to loss of jobs, housing, and friendships and could even jeopardize their personal safety. Billye Talmadge, who was studying to become a teacher in California in the early 1950s, put it like this in Eric Marcus's book *Making Gay History*: "At the time there was a list of about twenty-one things that you could lose your teaching certificate for. The first one was to be a card-carrying Communist, and the second was to be a homosexual. . . . And not only would you never teach in California, you would never teach again in public schools anywhere."[60]

ORGANIZE!

Gay activists were determined to fight against prejudice and gain the equal rights they had been denied. Following Stonewall, in July 1969, gay activists formed the Gay Liberation Front (GLF), a loosely organized group without leaders, to continue the protest against police brutality and other issues affecting the gay community. The GLF also participated in protests for civil rights for blacks and women and protests against the Vietnam War. A year after Stonewall, the GLF, led by Brenda Howard, a local bisexual activist, organized the Christopher Street Gay Liberation Day March through downtown New York City. Howard, nicknamed "the Mother of Pride," was determined that gay men and lesbians come out and declare themselves. Held on Sunday, June 28, 1970, exactly one year after Stonewall, the march was a protest against prejudice and discrimination. Similar marches took place in Los Angeles and San Francisco, starting an annual tradition. Today, the event is called the Gay Pride Parade. To be able to march through the streets of major cities symbolized the start of a new era. A new sense of identity took hold. By coming together and supporting each other, members of the gay community were able to be honest about their sexual identity and start pushing for equal rights and recognition.

Wanting to form a one-issue organization, some activists broke off from the GLF and formed the Gay Activists Alliance. One of their tactics was to stage outrageous events to draw public attention. Often, they approached public figures on the street. "We lay in wait for Mayor Lindsay to come out of the Metropolitan Museum and then stormed up the steps and got right in front of him and asked him embarrassing things,"[61] recalled Kay Lahusen, a reporter for gay newspapers. The group tried to organize gays as a voting block to influence elections, handing out leaflets in Bloomingdale's department store, stating where political candidates stood on gay issues.

DISCRIMINATION

Gays and lesbians may have begun to feel more open about themselves, yet they still faced discrimination in jobs, housing, government, the military, and other parts of daily life. Laws restricting homosexual activity were on the books in most states. Even without laws, employers felt free to fire homosexuals, and landlords to kick them out of housing, for no reason but their sexual orientation. Like women, blacks, and other identity groups, homosexuals began advocating for equal rights and protection under the law.

Gradually, states overturned old laws that discriminated against gays and passed new laws to protect gays and bisexuals. In 1982, Wisconsin was the first state that outlawed discrimination on the basis of sexual orientation. Other states passed similar laws. The medical establishment's view of homosexuality also changed. In 1973, the American Psychiatric Association removed homosexuality from its list of mental disorders.

Like other groups, gays founded legal organizations to fight for their rights. In 1973, gay rights advocates in New York City formed the Lambda Legal Defense Fund. The lowercase lambda, which is the eleventh letter of the Greek alphabet, is a popular symbol for the gay rights movement. A pioneer in tackling the legal issues that affect gays and lesbians in everyday life, Lambda took on many important civil rights cases. One of Lambda Legal's biggest victories was a case that overturned a Texas law prohibiting private consensual sex between two adults of the same sex. The case involved two men in Texas. Police entered their home mistakenly, discovered them in their bedroom, and arrested them because Texas had a law prohibiting sodomy, or sex between homosexuals.

In 2003, the U.S. Supreme Court ruled in *Lawrence v. Texas* that the Fourteenth Amendment protects private consensual sex between homosexuals. Writing for the Court majority, Justice Anthony Kennedy stated: "The petitioners are entitled to respect for their private lives.

The state cannot demean their existence or control their destiny by making their private sexual conduct a crime."[62] The Supreme Court's ruling applied not just to Texas but also to a dozen other states with similar laws, marking a major victory for gay rights. "This is a giant leap forward to a day where we are no longer branded as criminals,"[63] said Ruth Harlow, an attorney for the plaintiff and legal director of Lambda Legal.

BACKLASH FROM THE MORAL MAJORITY

Meanwhile, a backlash was building against the gay rights movement by conservative and evangelical Christians who believe homosexuality is a lifestyle choice and a sin, rather than a person's inborn identity. In 1977, Anita Bryant, a conservative singer, launched a drive to repeal a new gay rights ordinance in Dade County, Florida. The law banned discrimination against homosexuals in housing, employment, and public accommodation. Arguing that the law sent a message of approval about homosexuality, which she considered a sin, Bryant rallied 3,000 volunteers and the support of religious leaders in her crusade. Even major newspapers such as the *Miami Herald* sided with Bryant. Gay rights groups tried to fight against Bryant's crusade, but they failed to convince voters, and the law was overturned by a 2-to-1 majority in a county election. Bryant held a victory party. "The normal majority have said, 'Enough! Enough! Enough! Tonight, the laws of God and the cultural values of men have been vindicated,'"[64] she said.

Two years later, conservative and religious activists, led by the Reverend Jerry Falwell of Virginia, formed the Moral Majority, a conservative Christian organization that opposed abortion and gay rights. The outspoken Falwell pushed to get his platform adopted by the mainstream

Republican Party, then led by President Ronald Reagan, and he had some success. He tried to influence political decisions and turn back the tide of openness and civil rights for gays. "Please remember, homosexuals do not reproduce. They recruit! And many of them are out after my children and your children!"[65] Falwell wrote in a fundraising letter in 1981.

"LET THAT BULLET DESTROY EVERY CLOSET DOOR"

Violence against gays was still a dangerous possibility. In 1978, Harvey Milk, the first openly gay elected public official in the nation, was shot to death in San Francisco's city hall. A camera shop owner in San Francisco, Milk was a community organizer who was dishonorably discharged from the U.S. Navy after it was discovered he was gay. Nicknamed the "Mayor of Castor Street," for the street where he lived, Milk was charismatic and open about his gay identity. He lost three elections before he was voted to the Board of Supervisors for San Francisco in 1977.

Eleven months after he took office, on November 27, 1978, Milk was shot by a former city supervisor, Dan White. White had disagreed with Milk on many issues, including a new gay rights ordinance. After White resigned because of financial problems, he changed his mind and asked for his job back, but the mayor said no. Angry, White snuck into city hall with a gun. He first shot the mayor, George Moscone, and then turned his gun on Milk. Both victims died. White was convicted of two counts of voluntary manslaughter and given a seven-year, eight-month sentence. The light sentence may have resulted from what became known as the "Twinkie defense." White's lawyer argued the former fitness buff committed the crime because he was depressed and eating junk food, such as Twinkies and soda.

In 1978, Harvey Milk was the first openly gay elected public official in the United States when he was elected San Francisco's city supervisor. Milk is pictured here with San Francisco mayor George Moscone a year and a half before the two were assassinated by former city supervisor Dan White on November 27, 1978.

After White's sentence was handed down, the violent "White Night Riots" erupted in the city, with police cars burned and store windows smashed. Some 160 people were arrested, and many police and gay protestors were hospitalized. Harvey Milk became a symbol and a hero of the gay rights movement. Eerily, Milk had left a tape recording of a political will that was to be played in the event of his assassination. One of the statements on the tape was "If a bullet should enter my brain, let that bullet destroy every closet door." Later, after White was paroled after serving approximately six years of his sentence, he committed suicide.

In the face of the Milk murder and the Anita Bryant campaign to reverse gay rights, dozens of gay rights organizations pulled together to organize a massive march. On October 14, 1979, thousands of protestors gathered in the nation's capital for the National March on Washington for Lesbian and Gay Rights. They carried signs such as "My son is gay and that's okay" and "I served my country as a Gay American and I demand my rights." Once again, they were not giving up the fight.

ANTIGAY VIOLENCE

Milk was one in a long list of gays and lesbians who made headlines as targets of antigay violence or what are considered hate or bias crimes. Hate crimes are criminal acts that intend to harm or intimidate people because of their race, ethnicity, sexual orientation, religion, or other minority group status. The FBI reported in *Hate Crime Statistics 2005* that out of 8,804 victims of hate crimes, 1,213 of the victims were attacked because of sexual orientation. All but 23 of those individuals were attacked because they were perceived as gay, lesbian, or bisexual.

Since the 1980s, many states have responded with new anti-hate crime laws. According to the Lambda Gay and Lesbian Anti-Violence Project, 47 states and the District of Columbia have laws against hate crimes. Just 29 of those states and the District of Columbia include crimes based on the sexual orientation of the victim in their hate crimes statutes. No federal law covers hate crimes based on sexual orientation, though hate crimes due to the race, religion, color, and national origin of the victim are covered. Getting a federal hate crime statute that includes sexual orientation of the victim is a major goal of many gay and lesbian activist groups.

EPIDEMIC

The gay rights movement faced a new, devastating, challenge. In June 1981, the U.S. Centers for Disease Control and Prevention (CDC) reported that a rare form of pneumonia had been found in a small number of young gay men in Los Angeles. The pneumonia was later determined to be acquired immune deficiency syndrome, or AIDS, a wasting disease caused by a virus that attacks and disables the body's immune system so that it cannot fend off infections. The virus was identified as the human immunodeficiency virus, or HIV. Still with no known treatments, much less a cure, HIV/AIDS swept through the gay community in the 1980s. "AIDS, the experts said, was spreading rapidly. The number of cases was increasing geometrically, doubling every ten months, and the threat to heterosexuals appeared to be growing,"[66] wrote Claudia Wallis in a cover story in *Time* magazine in 1985. She reported that 6,000 people had already died of the disease, and an equal number were ill.

The public was gripped by fear and hysteria over the deadly disease, nicknamed the "gay plague," fueling new stigmas against gay men. The gay rights movement had opened doors, but the fear of AIDS reinforced the social marginalization of gays and the sense that gay behavior is not acceptable. Many people worried mistakenly that they could "catch" AIDS through casual contact and exposure; thus, they wanted to stay away from gays. The fear fueled a mistaken sense that AIDS was somehow shameful and perhaps even a punishment for immoral behavior. People were kicked out of their apartments and fired from jobs. Firemen did not want to resuscitate gay accident victims. A New York doctor was given an eviction notice by his co-op board because he was treating AIDS patients in his office in the building. "I treated people with AIDS. People in the building didn't like AIDS patients walking through the lobby,"[67] Dr. Joseph Sonnabend told *Time*.

"A MOTHER'S PLEA"

"Gay Man Beaten and Left For Dead; 2 Are Charged" was the *New York Times* headline on October 10, 1998.* Matthew Shepard, a 22-year-old openly gay student at the University of Wyoming in Laramie, had been left for dead on the side of the road, tied to a fence. Police soon suspected he was the victim of a hate crime. Two men at the local Fireside Bar had targeted him because he was gay, lured him to their truck, beat him, and left him. He died several days later. The two men were later convicted of felony murder and given two consecutive life sentences each. The news of Shepard's death incited both outrage and a reexamination of attitudes toward homosexuality. The tragedy sparked nationwide protests against hate crimes and anti-gay violence, and new anti-hate crime legislation in Congress. People in Laramie did not sound surprised. "If I were a homosexual in Laramie, I would hang low, very low. Openly gay behavior is not only discouraged, it's dangerous,"** Carla Brown, manager of the Fireside, told the *New York Times*.

Matthew's mother, Judy Shepard, put aside her grief and her family's privacy, and became an outspoken advocate for gay rights and stopping hate crimes. She testified before Congress in favor of a federal anti-hate crime law to protect gays. She and her husband, Dennis, started the Matthew Shepard Foundation in 1998 to help promote tolerance for gays and lesbians and fight against hate crimes. "Hate

Much-admired public figures who came forward as AIDS patients helped people realize the disease could touch anyone. In 1985, the Hollywood favorite Rock Hudson was the first actor to say that he had AIDS, putting a human face on the deadly disease. Other AIDS victims, such as Los Angeles Lakers' star Earvin "Magic" Johnson and tennis hero Arthur Ashe, both of whom spoke about their illness, also opened people's eyes. Magic Johnson held a press conference in November 1991 to announce that he would retire from basketball because of HIV. "I think sometimes we think; well, is a learned value. But you can unlearn it too—and that's really what we're trying to communicate to people."*** she said in a *Newsweek* interview.

She also travels to college campuses, where she sometimes begins her talks with a video showing images of the Ku Klux Klan, the lynching of blacks, the Holocaust, and children shouting "fag." She believes society still tolerates prejudice against gays; for example, teachers and parents often turn a blind eye to children using anti-gay slurs. Shepard encourages young people to respect others and speak out against injustice. She also asks students not to hide their sexual preferences but to be forthcoming about their identities. If they are open about who they are, acceptance will follow, said Shepard. "You can't convince society the gay community is harmless if you don't help show its true side,"† she told students at Boston College.

---

* James Brooke, "Gay Man Beaten and Left for Dead; 2 Are Charged," *New York Times*, October 10, 1998.

** Ibid.

*** Jessica Bennett, "A Call to Action." *Newsweek* online, December 8, 2006. Available online at *http://www.msnbc.msn. com/id/16116604/site/newsweek/*

† Natasha Reilly, "Judy Shepard Shares Son's Story," *Boston College Heights*, March 26, 2002.

only gay people can get it—'It's not going to happen to me.' And here I am saying that it can happen to anybody, even me, Magic Johnson,"[68] he said.

Along with advocating for more research and medical funds to fight HIV/AIDS, the gay community pulled together to protect itself. They formed local community groups to support AIDS victims on many fronts, from civil rights issues to access to health services and palliative care, or comfort and relief from the strains of illness. The Gay Men's Health Crisis (GMHC) opened in New York City in

1982 to provide therapy, phone crisis services, as well as financial and legal help. The GMHC also started a buddy program. People volunteered to help AIDS patients in daily tasks, such as cooking, shopping, and cleaning. They provided human contact to people who might have lost touch with their families due to the stigma of AIDS, even while they were dying.

AIDS ACTIVISM

In 1978, a group of gay activists concerned about the slow progress in the fight against AIDS met at the Lesbian and Gay Community Services Center in Manhattan and formed ACT UP, or the AIDS Coalition to Unleash Power. They decided to use nonviolent direct action campaigns to draw attention to the epidemic. On March 24, 1987, ACT UP held its first demonstration: a protest on Wall Street in front of Trinity Church to demand quicker government approval of AIDS drugs. Seventeen people who crossed the barricades and flooded the streets were arrested during the demonstration. More protests followed, and ACT UP became a noisy, visible reminder of the epidemic. On October 11, 1988, ACT UP, joined by the national ACT NOW coalition, closed down the Food and Drug Administration building outside of Washington, D.C. More than 1,000 activists staged a series of demonstrations, which result in almost 180 arrests. The event received international press coverage.

Gradually, with advocacy by the gay rights movement and others, the public realized that HIV/AIDS was not a "gay plague" but a disease that could strike anyone. Health education on preventing the transmission of AIDS spread as far as elementary schools. People realized that they could not "catch" AIDS through casual contact, and that they could prevent the spread of AIDS by taking simple precautionary steps, such as practicing safe sex and using condoms. Discrimination against people with HIV/AIDS, and by connection, gay men, gradually lessened.

In 1987, Cleve Jones, a gay rights activist in San Francisco, and his friends were looking for a way to memorialize friends and lovers who died of AIDS. They decided to start a quilt project to commemorate AIDS victims. People contributed colorful personal blocks and panels, which were sewn together, and the quilt grew. The Project AIDS Memorial Quilt became a fundraiser for AIDS programs, and the quilt was displayed throughout the country. In 1996, the quilt went on display in Washington, D.C. By then, the quilt was so large that it covered the entire National Mall. By 2007, the AIDS Memorial Quilt included more than 44,000 panels, and it was still growing. The quilt is a symbol of the healing process in the face of an epidemic that is still taking lives. More than three decades after its discovery, AIDS still has no cure, but treatment with a combination of antiretroviral drugs and regular access to primary healthcare are allowing people to live long and productive lives.

GAYS IN THE MILITARY

U.S. Air Force Technical Sergeant Leonard Matlovich was a model soldier. He served three tours of duty in Vietnam and won the Bronze Star, Purple Heart, and an Air Force Commendation Medal. He was also gay. In March 1975, Matlovich challenged the homosexual ban in the armed forces by writing a letter to his commanding officer: "I have arrived at the conclusion that my sexual preferences are homosexual, as opposed to heterosexual."[69] Despite his exemplary service record, the air force began efforts to discharge Matlovich. The sergeant became a central figure in the debate about whether gays should be in the military. Matlovich sued the air force. In 1980, a federal judge ordered

In 1987, gay rights activist Cleve Jones decided to create a quilt to commemorate friends and colleagues who had died from AIDS. Today, the quilt is the world's largest community arts project and memorializes more than 85,000 Americans who have died from AIDS. Here, the quilt is on display at the National Mall, in Washington, D.C., on October 11, 1996.

the air force to reinstate Matlovich, but Matlovich agreed to a $160,000 settlement instead. He died of AIDS in 1988. His tomb in the Congressional Cemetery in Washington, D.C., reads: "When I was in the military, they gave me a medal for killing two men and a discharge for loving one."

Homosexual behavior has long been cause for dismissal from the military. The argument used to justify this policy is the fear that gay soldiers will disrupt the cohesion of a military unit and undermine military performance. Cohesion means the forces that bind together the members of a group. During World War II, enlistees had to undergo psychiatric screening, and homosexuals were considered to be unfit for service. In the 1970s, gays pressed for civil rights in the military, and the issue seemed to be a matter of discretion. In 1981, the U.S. Department of Defense issued a new policy that banned gays from serving in the military. Thousands of gays were discharged during the next decade.

Gay groups fought the ban. Some of the men and women who had been discharged came out and protested. Gays in the military became the subject of a heated national debate. President Bill Clinton wanted to end the ban against gays in the military, but conservative members of Congress were not ready to go that far. A fierce political battle ensued. In 1993, President Clinton and Congress came up with a compromise policy, known as "Don't Ask, Don't Tell, Don't Pursue." The policy meant that the military does not allow openly gay people to serve in any of its branches, but it permits homosexuals who keep their sexual orientation secret to enlist and serve. Gay advocacy groups did not like the policy: They wanted an antidiscrimination policy instead. In fact, dismissals of gay soldiers rose after the new policy was enacted, and harassment and discrimination continued. In 1999, a gay soldier at Fort Campbell, Kentucky, was beaten to death with a baseball bat, after being harassed for months.

"THE HAPPIEST DAY OF OUR LIVES"

On May 17, 2004, Hillary and Julie Goodridge were the first in a long line of people gathered at the city hall in downtown Boston, waiting to make history. On that day, Massachusetts became the first state to legalize same-sex marriage, the result of a lawsuit known as *Goodridge v. Department of Public Health.* The plaintiffs in the case were seven same-sex couples, including the Goodridges who had been together for 13 years and had a five-year-old daughter. They wanted to publicly affirm their commitment to each other and get the legal protections and benefits of married couples. In its decision, the Massachusetts Supreme Judicial Court ruled that it was unconstitutional for the state to allow only heterosexual couples to marry. "The Massachusetts Constitution affirms the dignity and equality of all individuals. It forbids the creation of second-class citizens. In reaching our conclusion we have given full deference to the arguments made by the Commonwealth. But it has failed to identify any constitutionally adequate reason for denying civil marriage to same-sex couples,"[70] stated the 2003 court decision.

After they received their marriage license, the Goodridges talked to reporters. "Next to the birth of our daughter, Annie, this is the happiest day of our lives," said Julie Goodridge. When Hillary was asked what she would tell the opponents of gay marriage, she replied, "Come on over to our house for dinner and find out how loving and normal and boring we are."[71] Despite the exhilaration of that day, the controversy about same-sex marriage, or the union of two persons of the same sex who live as a family, was far from over. The day that same-sex marriage became legal in Massachusetts, President George W. Bush spoke out strongly against it. "The sacred institution of marriage should not be redefined by a few activist judges,"[72] he stated. In 2004, he proposed an amendment to the U.S. Constitution to define marriage as the union between a man and a woman. Changing the Constitution would prove to be difficult, and Congress did not go along with his idea.

Legalizing the partnerships of same-sex couples is controversial because it involves many basic issues that deal with family, children, community, and religion. To gay and lesbian couples, the right to marry, or at least have a civil union, is a fundamental right that they feel has been wrongfully denied to them. Married couples have many legal privileges not available to those who are unmarried, such as shared healthcare benefits, the transfer of property, tax benefits, and overall security. Advocates of same-sex marriage argue the institution provides stability for the family and community, and especially the children in these homes. Opponents believe just as strongly that only a man and a woman should be allowed to marry. They say that same-sex marriage undermines the concept of marriage, which involves conceiving children, and that allowing gays to marry would change what marriage means. Some opponents raise religious objections, while others point to social issues. "If we have homosexual marriage mainstream, I can't even describe to you what our culture will be like,"[73] said Sandy Rios, president of Concerned Women for America, an anti-gay marriage organization.

In 1996, President Bill Clinton signed the Defense of Marriage Act, which prevents the federal government from recognizing same-sex marriage and gives states the right to ignore same-sex marriage licenses from other states. Some 45 states also have laws or constitutional restrictions against same-sex marriage. A handful of states has moved forward with same-sex civil unions or domestic partnerships, offering many of the legal rights as marriage. In 1999, Vermont was the first state to recognize civil unions between same-sex

Vermont became the first U.S. state to recognize civil unions between same-sex couples in 1999, when the Vermont Supreme Court ruled in *Baker v. Vermont* that same-sex couples should have the same rights that heterosexual couples enjoy. Pictured here are the three couples who brought the case against the state. Clockwise: Stacey Jolles, Nina Beck, Peter Harrigan, Stan Baker, Lois Farnham, and Holly Puterbaugh.

couples. Couples in civil unions are entitled to the same benefits and responsibilities as heterosexual couples, but they are not "married." California has a same-sex partnership law giving couples many of the benefits of married couples. Approximately 30,000 same-sex couples were registered as domestic partners in California in 2006, according to the *Los Angeles Times.* In September 2006, the California State Assembly went a step further and passed the Religious Freedom and Civil Marriage Protection Act. The law changes the definition of marriage from between a man and a woman to between "two persons."

Early on February 19, 2007, gay and lesbian couples gathered at city halls throughout New Jersey to apply for civil unions. New Jersey had become the third state, after Vermont and Connecticut, to offer civil unions. Steven Goldstein and Daniel Gross of Teaneck were the first couple given the state's legal right of a civil union. Teaneck deputy mayor Lizette Parker asked, "Do you, Steven, agree to be legally joined with Daniel under the Civil Union Law of the state of New Jersey?" Goldstein replied, "I do."[74] Still, both men were determined to keep working toward the next step: the day New Jersey legalizes marriage between two men or two women. "Nothing short of marriage will do,"[75] said Gross.

GROWING UP GAY

In 1996, comedian Ellen DeGeneres approached the Disney executives who produced *Ellen*, the prime-time ABC comedy in which she starred. She wanted her character Ellen Morgan to come out as a lesbian. This would be a big step for DeGeneres, for she would be coming out, too. Throughout her career as a stand-up comedian and sitcom star, she had kept her personal life a secret. "It's hard enough to get them to like you when you're a girl on stage. . . . I knew it was going to be impossible to get them to like me if they knew I was gay,"[76] said DeGeneres. The executives agreed to the new plot, but they put a warning label on the show about adult material. After Ellen Morgan came out on prime time, the show's ratings dropped sharply. DeGeneres received hate mail and bad reviews in the press. The show was cancelled after the next season. Still, DeGeneres bounced back. In 2003, she launched a daytime talk show, *The Ellen DeGeneres Show*, and by 2007, she was hosting the Academy Awards. "I didn't feel like I had a choice and I didn't think of the consequences. It's like seeing somebody drowning in the river and you jump in. You're kind of aware it's a dangerous thing to do, but you've got to do it,"[77] she said.

Outside the spotlight, the process of coming out is not any easier. In high schools throughout the country, where approximately 5 percent of students identify themselves as gay, lesbian, or bisexual, teens still struggle with their identities. Studies show that gay teens are at a higher risk for suicide than other teens, in part because the harassment and bullying they often encounter, which can lead to depression and anxiety. Four out of five gay teens hear homophobic remarks often at school, and 39 percent have been verbally or physically assaulted, according to the Gay, Lesbian and Straight Education Network (GLSEN), a national advocacy and education organization.

Today, many teens discover there is help out there. Web sites, teen help phone lines, blogs, and magazines reach out to gay teens. At least 3,000 high schools have set up Gay-Straight Alliances, or GSAs, which are student-run clubs that give teens a safe place to talk about issues relating to sexual orientation and how to end homophobia. The GLSEN helps schools set up GSAs, along with antibullying policies, while encouraging gay teens to become involved. "The most important step to take is to empower yourself," said GLSEN founder and executive director Kevin Jennings. "The real battle for gay people is not winning an election or getting a policy passed. It's the battle for visibility. So the minute you speak out for your rights, you've won a major part of the battle."[78]

7

American Indians Reclaim Pride

The year was 1973 and the place was Wounded Knee, a wind-swept settlement on the sprawling Pine Ridge Reservation in southwestern South Dakota. Stretching over grassy plains, pine hills, and badlands, Pine Ridge Reservation is the home of the Oglala Lakota (Sioux) Nation, where many families in the 1970s lived in tar-paper shacks without running water or electricity and the average yearly income was $900. On February 27 of that year, some 300 American Indians, led by local Lakotas and leaders of the American Indian Movement (AIM) took over Wounded Knee, which had a trading post, a few churches, and several houses. They refused to leave until a commission was formed to review the 1868 treaty establishing the Sioux homeland. The protestors also demanded that the Bureau of Indian Affairs, the federal agency overseeing reservations, allow new elections to replace the allegedly corrupt Pine Ridge tribal council. For 71 days, they occupied the town, surrounded by armed federal marshals.

The site of the last major confrontation between American Indians and federal soldiers, Wounded Knee already held a dark place in history. On a frigid December night in 1890, federal soldiers killed approximately 300 Sioux men, women, and children on the banks of Wounded Knee Creek, marking the end of the nineteenth-century Indian wars. By then, tribes throughout the country had been driven off their ancestral land; many, like the Sioux, were hungry and homeless. The Sioux partook a spiritual revival called the Ghost Dance, but the U.S. government tried to quash it. Afterward, one of the generals, Nelson A. Miles, described the scene as "a massacre." Others saw it as even worse. "A people's dream died there. It was a beautiful dream . . . the nation's hoop is broken and scattered. There is no center any longer, and the sacred tree is dead,"[79] wrote Black Elk, the Oglala Lakota holy man.

Now, in 1973, journalists poured into Pine Ridge Reservation to report on the siege. The standoff at Wounded Knee shone a spotlight on the grievances of American Indians, who complained of racism, powerlessness, and life controlled by a federal bureaucracy. Many people sympathized with the protestors, but they worried about violence. "More Indian martyrs, more Indian blood on white man's hands, can serve no purpose but to unify divided Indians in further and stronger defiance of the white man's rule that has so consistently cheated and degraded them,"[80] wrote *New York Times* reporter Tom Wicker. Both sides were armed and traded fire. Before the occupation ended on May 8, 1973, two of the occupiers, Frank Clearwater and Buddy Lamont, were killed and two FBI agents and a federal marshal were wounded. Not much was gained by the protest, which lasted from February 27 to May 8, 1973, but Wounded Knee proved that American Indians would be seen and heard. Change was in the wind.

PRIDE IN IDENTITY

A long history of loss and broken pride propelled this civil rights movement bent on restoring American Indian identity and self-determination. For much of the twentieth century, tribal leaders had worked cooperatively with the Bureau of Indian Affairs, which managed the reservations and provided services to tribal members. However, by the 1960s, American Indians had grown impatient. They wanted more self-government and *tribal sovereignty*, or independent rule, and respect for historic treaty and land rights. They wanted better housing, job opportunities, and improved education on the hundreds of tribal reservations in the United States. The Red Power movement set out to restore the dignity of American Indians.

Torn between old traditions and modern society, American Indians were struggling to maintain their culture. About half of tribal members lived on reservations, most of which were established in the nineteenth century after tribes were forced off their land and made to live under federal jurisdiction on smaller parcels. In exchange for the land, the government promised to provide for the health, safety, and welfare of the native people, but the results were discouraging. With substandard housing and schools, poor health services, and few economic opportunities, by the 1960s many reservations offered little prospect for the future, fueling alcoholism and other social problems. The infant mortality rate was twice the national average, and the average age of death was under 50 years. "What happens to an Indian child who is forced to abandon his own pride and future and confront a society in which he has been offered neither a place nor a hope!"[81] stated Senator Edward M. Kennedy (D-Massachusetts), chairman of the Special Subcommittee on Indian Education in 1969. In addition, hundreds of historic treaties protecting tribal land and resources had been broken by the U.S. government.

Frustration festered, and a rebellious spirit took hold. Nearly half of American Indians had moved to cities by the 1960s, and some young people were in college, where they were inspired by the civil rights and antiwar movements. In

1961, students in Gallup, New Mexico, formed the National Indian Youth Council (NIYC). One of the leaders was Clyde Warrior, a Ponca activist, who said that no assistance programs would help American Indians until they took pride in their identity—a revolutionary idea at that time. The NIYC set out to restore the historic fishing rights held by the tribes in the Pacific Northwest. The coastal tribes had been pushed off their fishing grounds, despite treaties protecting their rights.

SPIRIT WARRIORS

In 1968, a group of community activists in Minneapolis, Minnesota, led by Dennis Banks, Clyde Bellecourt, and several others, formed the American Indian Movement to protest what they saw as racism and abuse by police toward tribal members. AIM soon took on other issues. Several AIM leaders had confrontations with the law, but they saw a chance to return to their traditional religion, regain tribal identities, and push for treaty rights. "Before AIM, Indians were dispirited, defeated, and culturally dissolving. People were ashamed to be Indian. You didn't see the young people wearing braids or chokers or ribbon shirts in those days. . . . We put Indians and Indian rights smack dab in the middle of the public consciousness for the first time since the so-called Indian wars,"[82] said Russell Means, an Oglala Sioux and early member of AIM, in a PBS interview. Means later broke with AIM.

As self-described warriors, AIM leaders wore traditional braids and beads. They sought the advice of spiritual tribal elders and brought drums and pipes to demonstrations. In November 1972, AIM organized the Trail of Broken Treaties, bringing more than 2,000 American Indians to Washington, D.C., to urge President Richard Nixon to respond to 20 demands on issues such as education, treaties,

"WE ARE NOT FREE"

As part of his War on Poverty, a national effort to stem poverty in the United States through programs like Head Start and food stamps, President Lyndon B. Johnson formed the National Advisory Commission on Rural Poverty in 1966. The commission held three public hearings to gather information on rural poverty, including one in Memphis, Tennessee, in February 1967. At the Memphis hearing, a young Native American activist named Clyde Warrior stood up to speak. Warrior, a Ponca Indian from Oklahoma, was one of the founders of the National Indian Youth Council, a radical organization that sought self-determination for American Indians. His speech became one of the most important statements on the native issues in the 1960s. This is part of it:

We are not free. We do not make choices. Our choices are made for us; we are the poor. For those of us who live on reservations these choices and decisions are made by federal administrators, bureaucrats, and their "yes men," euphemistically called tribal governments. Those of us who live in non-reservation areas have our lives controlled by local white power elites. We have many rulers. They are called social workers, "cops," school teachers, churches, etc. . . . They call us into meetings to tell us what is good for us and how they've programmed us, or they come into our homes to instruct us and their manners are not always what one would call polite by Indian standards or perhaps by any standards. We are rarely accorded respect as fellow human beings. Our children come home from school to us with shame in their hearts and a sneer on their lips for their home and parents. We are the "poverty problem" and that is true; and perhaps it is also true that our lack of reasonable choices, our lack of freedoms, our poverty of spirit is not unconnected with our material poverty.[*]

---

[*] Wayne Moquin and Charles Van Doren, eds., *Great Documents in American Indian History* (New York: Da Capo Press, 1995), 355–356.

American Indians continue to protest the unfair treatment they have received from the U.S. government. Here, former AIM leaders Dennis Banks (left) and Clyde Bellecourt beat a drum during a rally at South Dakota's Pine Ridge Reservation in July 1999 to protest the most recent in a long line of unsolved murders at the reservation.

health, and water rights. For seven days, they occupied the Bureau of Indian Affairs headquarters. Forceful actions like this one made AIM controversial, but people took notice. "We may disagree with their tactics, but there's not a single Indian organization anywhere that would disagree with those twenty points. A lot of Indians out there are watching the protest and saying 'right on!'"[83] said one native observer during the takeover.

Still, violence marred the movement. After Wounded Knee, FBI agents continued to patrol Pine Ridge, creating tension and resentment among residents there. On June 26, 1975, a shoot-out between Indians and FBI agents in Oglala, South Dakota, resulted in the deaths of two agents and one American Indian. AIM leader Leonard Peltier was convicted of murdering the two agents, and he is serving two consecutive life sentences, though he continues to proclaim his innocence. "I swear to you, I am guilty only of being an Indian. That's why I'm here,"[84] he wrote in his memoir. His imprisonment became a rallying cause for human rights organizations throughout the world, and he became a martyr for the movement, but Peltier hoped for more. "We were spirit-warriors, not mercenaries. We wanted peace, not conflict,"[85] Peltier wrote.

OCCUPATION OF ALCATRAZ

AIM was not the only group fighting for native rights. In November 1969, a coalition of urban Indians, students, activists, and tribal leaders, calling themselves the Indians of All Tribes, boarded boats to Alcatraz Island in San Francisco Bay. Before Spanish settlers colonized California, Alcatraz was a sacred place for coastal Indian tribes. In 1934, Alcatraz became a maximum security federal prison, but by 1964, the land was federal surplus property and the buildings were abandoned. The activists wanted the land returned to the Indians of All Tribes, with plans to create a center for American Indian education and culture.

Up to 1,000 people, including families with children, camped without sanitation and medical care in the crumbling buildings. They danced, built fires, talked into the night, and got their message out through the media. The conditions were terrible, and their determination frayed. The 12-year-old daughter of one leader fell and died. Still, the group stayed on Alcatraz for 19 months, refusing to leave until they got the island back. In the end, they received a lot of publicity, but their demands were unanswered. Still, to many, the occupation was significant. "Alcatraz was symbolic in the rebirth of Indian people to be recognized as a people, as human beings, whereas before, we were not,"[86] said Dr. LaNada Boyer, a Shoshone-Bannock who was a leader of the occupation, in a PBS interview.

SELF-DETERMINATION

Even though the sit-ins and takeovers did not always achieve immediate goals, the pressure from the activists spurred Congress to take important steps toward improving the status of American Indians with new legislation such as the Indian Civil Rights Act of 1968, which guaranteed defendants basic civil rights in tribal courts. In 1972, the Indian Education Act established the Office of Indian Education and an advisory council on education. In the past, native children educated in government schools were forced to give up their customs and assimilate to white culture. Schools on reservations were substandard and underfunded; only a tiny percentage of students made it to college. The U.S. government acknowledged native students needed appropriate educational services and more funding. In the late 1970s, lawmakers passed dozens of other laws that helped American Indians regain water, fishing, and land rights. New laws that strengthened the tribes' ability to govern themselves were also approved.

Still, demonstrations continued. On July 15, 1978, hundreds of American Indians streamed into Washington, D.C., on the last leg of a 3,500-mile walk from California, which began the previous February. Led by tribal elders, they gathered around the Reflecting Pool near the Capitol and passed a peace pipe. "We are here to let America know that everything hasn't been given away, that everything hasn't been stolen from us, that we are still a way of life that survives,"[87] Clyde Bellecourt told the *New York Times*. The Longest Walk was taken, in part, to protest legislation before Congress that threatened reservations. Since World War II, the United States had followed a "termination policy" to reduce federal support of reservations and encourage American Indians to leave their land and assimilate into white culture. New legislation before Congress would have carried on this policy, but it was dropped soon after. Now the push was on to improve lives on the reservations.

RELIGIOUS FREEDOM

One of the most important fights was for religious freedom. Historically, the federal government tried to "civilize" American Indians by converting them to Christianity. The 1887 Dawes Act prohibited spiritual ceremonies such as the Sun Dance. At mission schools, where native children were sent to be educated, traditional religions were banned. Now, with pressure from activists, Congress was compelled to respond. The American Indian Religious Freedom Act of 1978 guaranteed American Indians the right to practice their religion with traditional ceremonies in sacred places. With this new law, native religious practices, including sacred sites and objects, were protected by the First Amendment for the first time.

Still, religious issues persisted, such as the right to use peyote, an illegal drug, in sacred ceremonies. In a setback for American Indians, the Supreme Court ruled in 1990 that states can decide whether to permit the use of illegal drugs for religious purposes. In this case, *Employment Division of Oregon v. Smith*, two American Indians in Oregon lost their jobs and unemployment benefits because they used peyote for religious purposes. Unwilling to let that ruling stand, three years later, Congress passed the Religious Freedom Restoration Act, allowing natives to bypass drug laws for religious purposes. However, the debate continues.

The hunting of eagles for tribal ceremonies is also controversial. Although eagles are a protected species, American Indians are allowed to use eagle feathers for spiritual purposes, but only those secured from a federal repository in Colorado. In 2005, a Northern Arapaho man was arrested for killing a bald eagle in Wyoming for an Arapaho Sun Dance. A federal judge ruled in 2006 that the preservation of Indian tribes and culture was more important than protecting the eagle in this case. "This is an important ruling because it emphasizes the sanctity of the Sun Dance and the obligation of the Arapaho people to nurture our sacred ceremonies for future generations,"[88] Nelson White Sr., a Northern Arapaho Business Council member, told the *Casper Star-Tribune*.

In 1990, the Native American Graves Protection and Repatriation Act provided protection for tribal graves and remains. Yet it would be difficult for Indian tribes to lay claim to objects and sites that were no longer theirs. Under the new law, five Indian tribes attempted to claim the bones of a 9,000-year-old human, named the Kennewick Man, discovered in 1996 on federal lands near the Columbia River in Washington. The tribes believed he was their ancestor, but a federal magistrate in 2002 ruled that the bones should be turned over to scientists to study because the tribes were unable to prove a direct relationship. For now, the Kennewick Man, the property of the U.S. Army Corps of Engineers, is held at the Burke Museum at the University of Washington. Throughout the United States, many museums still display sacred objects and ancestral skeletal remains without tribal consent, violating the traditional belief that disturbing the dead interrupts their spiritual journeys.

REDSKINS AND TOMAHAWKS

Native activists have tried hard to put an end to stereotypes that ridicule American Indians, or alternately depict them as heroic and close to nature. "White people only like Indians if we're warriors or guardians of the earth,"[89] said author Sherman Alexie who grew up on the Spokane reservation and writes about contemporary American Indian. Stereotypes are damaging. Others echo that sense of the one-dimensional American Indians. In a 2006 interview with National Public Radio, Joe Day, who is married to a Hopi, and runs a gift shop on Second Mesa on Arizona's Hopi Reservation, put it like this: "White people tend to have two kinds of stereotypes about Indians. There's the drunken, thieving, lazy, savage stereotype. And there's the brown man living in harmony with his fellow man and with the environment. Everybody can see the evil in the first stereotype. But I think the second stereotype is just as evil, because stereotypes keep us from relating to people as people."[90] Stereotypes can lead to feelings of shame and inferiority on the part of natives and discrimination by non-Indians. A study by the U.S. Office of Housing and Urban Development in 2003 found that American Indians face more discrimination in rental housing than any minority group.

Starting in the late 1960s, activists tried to convince the Cleveland Indians baseball team to get rid of their mascot, Chief Wahoo, a cartoon-like red man with a big nose and buck teeth. The Cleveland team, which has yet to give up Chief Wahoo, is not alone. Many sports teams, from the Washington Redskins to the Marquette High School Redmen in Michigan, use Indian names, logos, and mascots. Fans at Atlanta Braves baseball games cheer their team with the tomahawk chop, waving foam tomahawks and chanting. Critics say the symbols and mascots are racist and portray Indians in negative one-dimensional ways. "Chief Wahoo

Both professional and amateur sports teams have used demeaning images of American Indians for mascots and logos for many years, but recently, organizations such as the NCAA have started to ban the use of these images. Here, Michael Hanley (speaking) of the National Coalition on Racism in Sports and the Media and Ken Rhyne (left) of the American Indian Movement talk with reporters during the 1995 World Series between the Atlanta Braves and Cleveland Indians.

offends Indian people the same way that Little Black Sambo offended African Americans and the Frito Bandito offended the Hispanic community and should have offended all of us. It assaults the principle of justice,"[91] stated Spokane artist and professor Charlene Teters, vice president of the National Coalition on Racism in Sports and Media. Others disagree, saying the Indian names and mascots promote team spirit and are not meant to disparage.

Some teams have changed their names. The University of Oklahoma dropped its "Little Red" mascot in 1970. Dartmouth, Stanford, Syracuse, St. John's, and Miami (Ohio) University all did away with their Indian mascots, too. Still, many teams are reluctant to give up popular mascots. In a victory for native activists, in 2005, the National Collegiate Athletic Association (NCAA) banned the use of Indian mascots that convey a negative image at postseason college championship games. "As a national association, we believe that mascots, nicknames or images deemed hostile or abusive in terms of race, ethnicity or national origin should not be visible at the championship events that we control,"[92] stated Walter Harrison, chair of the NCAA executive committee and the president of the University of Hartford. Schools face stiff penalties if they don't comply. "This is a big step in the right direction," said Tex Hall, president of the National Council on American Indians, in a press release. "The ridicule, mockery and utter racism Native Americans are subject to because of the use of Indian mascots are intolerable."[93]

CASINOS BRING WEALTH AND CONTROVERSY

By the 1980s, the revolutionary fervor had quieted, but the drive toward self-government, identity, and sovereignty was going strong. To fight poverty on many reservations, tribes looked for new business ventures. In 1988, Congress passed the Indian Regulatory Gaming Act, allowing federally recognized tribes to open casinos and gaming facilities on their land with state approval. Tribes saw gaming as an opportunity to end reliance on government subsidies and gain self-sufficiency. Throughout the country, dozens of casinos opened for business, creating new jobs and revenue on reservations.

The Mashantucket Pequot Tribal Nation in Connecticut had scattered and almost disappeared, but the tribe reestablished itself to open the Foxwoods Casino Resort in 1992, now a hugely successful venture that brings in more than $1 billion every year. The casino and its hotels, restaurants, theaters, and other businesses created thousands of jobs in a struggling Connecticut economy. Part of the profits went to build the Mashantucket Pequot Museum and Research Center to celebrate the Pequot culture and history. Still, people in nearby towns complain about the traffic, the casino expansion, and the fact that Indian-owned businesses do not have to abide by many state laws.

Not everyone thinks casinos are the answer to tribes' economic straits; instead, critics say, the presence of casinos encourage tribal members to waste their money gambling. Poverty endures on some remote reservations with casinos, such as Standing Rock Reservation in North and South Dakota, where the unemployment rate is high despite two casinos. Some tribes resisted casinos because of objections about large-scale gambling. The Navajo Nation voted down casinos twice before 2004, when the first Navajo casino was approved, but as of mid-2007, ground has yet to be broken for the casino. Also, questions are being asked about who benefits from and controls the tribal casinos. Non-Indian investors and lobbyists who finance and develop the casinos have reaped huge profits from the ventures, and many employees at casinos are not tribal members. Yet for the Pequot and dozens of other tribes, the new housing, schools, businesses, and cultural centers made possible by casino revenue have created a much brighter future.

"THEY SPOKE THE LANGUAGE"

One of the legacies of the Red Power movement is the revival of tribal culture and traditions—and a new celebration of native identity. Starting in the late 1960s, a creative renaissance bloomed in art, literature, film, and music. In the past, most books about American Indians were written by white writers, but today native writers are creating a new literature, and one that is diverse. Children's writer Joseph Bruchac, who is part Abenaki, and Spokane novelist Sherman Alexie, provide very different perspectives from the inside. Bruchac, who has written books on Sacajawea and Crazy Horse, often focuses on history and legends. Alexie writes about the everyday, often difficult, life of ordinary Indians in cities and on reservations. His gritty portrayals of poverty and alcoholism are sometimes controversial. "It's great to talk about traditions and to see them represented and to get a sense of history, but I think it's more important to change the possibilities of what an Indian is and can be right now. We're not separate, we're not removed, we're an integral and living part of the culture,"[94] Alexie said in an interview on Bookpage.com.

Acclaimed Acoma Pueblo poet Simon Ortiz grew up listening to his grandfather tell stories in the Acoma language. He learned the value of storytelling as a way to preserve cultural values and memory. Ortiz writes poetry about everyday life for Pueblos in New Mexico, showing their difficulties, but also celebrating their strength. He is a champion of native literature. "It's a form of resistance. If there was not a body of

American Indians have traditionally passed along their peoples'
stories and history to the next generation through word of mouth.
However, with the threat that some tribes' languages may be lost
forever, many American Indians have set about to preserve their
language. Pictured here is Acoma Pueblo poet Simon Ortiz, who is
helping to preserve the Pueblo language.

literature, then Native people would be invisible. Sometimes
the term 'Indian' is an abstract idea. But when we express
ideas in literature, then we have a valid body of expression
that's totally ours,"[95] Ortiz told CNN in 2004.

Ortiz is also helping preserve the Pueblo language, one
of many native languages in danger of extinction. In 1996,
only 175 native languages had survived, out of more than
300 before European colonization, according to the National
Indian Education Association. The association predicts that
the number could drop to 20 by 2050 unless more is done.
Language is an essential part of a group's identity, whether it is
American Sign Language for the deaf or Spanish for Latinos.
With the loss of language comes a further loss of identity as

a Navajo, Cherokee, or Lakota. "My grandparents—lived in extreme poverty, but they were proud of who they were. . . . They were proud of being Lakota. They spoke the language. They understood the ceremonies. They understood the culture. Poverty isn't what is causing our children to commit suicide. It's being lost in their identity,"[96] said Ron His Horse Is Thunder, chairman of the Standing Rock Sioux Tribe and a great-great-great-grandson of Sitting Bull, the great Sioux leader. Ron His Horse Is Thunder wants to bring the Lakota language back to everyday use at Standing Rock in the Dakotas, where a rash of teen suicides in recent years has plagued the reservation.

Inspired by the American Indian civil rights movement, tribes throughout the country set out to save languages no longer spoken by their children. Time was running out, because many languages were never written down. In some tribes, the language had already disappeared. In others, only a few older members could speak the words they learned as children. In the Oneida Nation of Wisconsin, where only a handful of older members spoke Oneida, language classes were begun in the schools. The Oneida didn't want to lose their language. A linguistics professor at the University of Wisconsin, Green Bay, named Clifford Abbott learned Oneida, taught adults classes on the reservation, and even edited an Oneida dictionary. Today, tribal child care centers and elementary and high schools have Oneida language classes. Tribal elders translated an English dictionary into Oneida and published a book of Oneida folk stories. Adults who had lost the Oneida words they learned from their grandparents have begun speaking the language again.

MANY CHALLENGES LAY AHEAD

The Red Power movement has left many other legacies. Tribal sovereignty and self-sufficiency are gaining strength at reservations throughout the country. Approximately 100 colleges and universities now have American Indian studies programs. The Smithsonian Institution's National Museum of the American Indian opened in Washington, D.C., in 2004. It is an important center for the understanding and celebration of native identity and culture. Yet balancing native identity and life in contemporary America is not easy. For example, on the Pine Ridge Reservation in South Dakota, site of the Wounded Knee standoff in 1973, the challenges are many. The reservation is the poorest region of the country, and residents cope with drug and alcohol addiction, a high student drop-out rate, unemployment reaching 80 percent, and lack of basic amenities, such as banks and libraries. Yet there is a pride that was not there before 1973. Many reservation jobs once held by whites are now held by Lakotas. New businesses have been established. "A lot of young people are identifying with their culture. You see a lot more Lakota culture practiced here now than before the movement came here,"[97] one tribal member told a reporter from the *Argus Leader* in Sioux Falls, South Dakota.

On February 28, 2003, people gathered at the cemetery in Wounded Knee to honor the thirtieth anniversary of the standoff. Even among the Oglala Lakota, divisive scars remain. Some people are still angry at AIM's takeover and the violence that ensued; others are proud to have been a part of it. Yet no one will forget it. A woman named Thunder Hawk recalled surviving the three blizzards that swept through Wounded Knee during the months of protest. "We made our stand. I knew modern day Indian history had been made," Thunder Hawk told the *Argus Leader*. "I didn't know how to articulate it. But I knew something had happened, and I was a part of it, and I didn't want it to end."[98]

8

Muslims in the United States after 9/11

A group of Muslim religious leaders was removed from a U.S. Airways plane waiting to take off from the Minneapolis–St. Paul International Airport in November 2006. Passengers had complained that three of the men were praying at the gate while waiting to board the plane. The incident created a national uproar, with people coming down on both sides of the issue. Some said that the Muslims were being religiously discriminated against. "This was humiliating, the worst moment of my life," one of men told the *Minneapolis Star Tribune.* "To practice your faith and pray is a crime in America?"[99] Others said that airplane officials cannot be too cautious when it comes to public safety.

Forging an Islamic identity in the United States became more challenging after September 11, 2001, when airplanes hijacked by 19 Muslim men flew into the Pentagon and the World Trade Center, killing 2,973 people, including the hijackers, with more than 20 more people still missing. Some of the victims were Muslims, and Muslims were among the many Americans who stepped forward to donate money and provide emergency assistance afterward. Still, overnight, Muslims in the United States began to experience suspicion and distrust, as though all of them were personally responsible for the tragic events. To them, Islam was a religion that meant submission to God and service to others, but, around them, Islam was portrayed as a religion of fanaticism and terror. Suddenly, they were living in fear, themselves. In Dallas, Texas, bullets flew through a local mosque in a drive-by shooting the day after 9/11. A radio DJ in Florida ranted about "towel heads" during his radio show.[100] Islamic organizations expressed both fear and outrage. "All too many people are blaming the innocent,"[101] said Marvin Wingfield of the American-Arab Anti-Discrimination Committee.

Sweeping antiterrorism laws passed after the September 11 attacks allowed the U.S. government more leeway to investigate and detain people suspected of terrorism. While officials defended the new laws as necessary for public safety, Muslim groups felt their constitutional rights were being infringed upon simply because of their religion or ethnicity. "I'm a Muslim woman who wears a scarf, a head scarf, but who I am is not an extremist or fundamentalist, it's someone who's trying to remember God in her life,"[102] said Ingrid Mattson, the first woman to be president of the Islamic Society of North America, one of the largest Islamic organizations in North America. The anti-Muslim sentiment did not ebb as time passed. A Cornell University poll in 2004 showed that nearly half of Americans polled believed that civil liberties of Muslims should be curtailed by the U.S. government. In February 2007, leaders of several Islamic mosques in New Jersey received anonymous threatening letters.

IDENTITY CRISIS

The September 11 attacks sparked an identity crisis for American Muslims, as they looked inside themselves to see what Islam meant to them and how to practice their religion in the United States. Parents wondered if they should send their children to religious schools in order to get a stronger background in Islam. Women worried about wearing *hijab*, the traditional head coverings worn by some Muslims. Muslims who grew up in the United States questioned if they should try harder to assimilate and hide their Islamic identity, or become more religious, traditional, and separate. "There is tension between conservative and more liberal or reform-minded Muslims focused mostly on openness to America. The differences are healthy. It shows the community is thinking and evolving. Muslims are going through a process of transition from being Muslims in America to being American Muslims,"[103] said Liyakat Takim, assistant professor of Islamic studies at the University of Denver. Non-Muslims were curious, too. Mosques and other Islamic organizations experienced more visitors looking for information about Islam. Never before had so many copies of the Quran, the Islamic holy book, been sold in the United States. A young Muslim Boy Scout echoed the feelings of many American Muslims. "We're just average American boys doing average American activities. But after Sept. 11, we also have to be ambassadors of our faith,"[104] said Rehman Muhammad, 13, a member of Houston's Troop 797.

Muslims are followers of Islam, the fastest growing religion in the world, practiced by about one-fifth of the world's population. The monotheistic religion was founded by the prophet Muhammad, born in the year 570 in Mecca, the land that is now Saudi Arabia. Muhammad was a poor trader who often meditated. When he was 40 years old, the angel Gabriel came to him with messages from Allah (God). The messages he received became the Quran, the Islamic sacred text, and Muhammad began teaching what he learned to others. By the time he died in 632, most of Arabia was under Muslim control and the religion soon spread as far as China and Spain. Today, Islam is centered in the Middle East and North Africa, but it is practiced in countries throughout the world. Most Arabs are Muslims, but only about 15 percent of the 1.2 billion Muslims in the world are Arabs. Many non-Arabic countries are predominately Muslim, including Indonesia and Pakistan.

Islam is not just a religion but a way of life. For example, Muslims keep dietary laws prohibiting then from drinking alcohol and eating pork. The Five Pillars of Islam are the basic aspects of carrying out the religion. They include bearing witness that there is no god but God and Muhammad is his prophet; performing five daily ritual prayers; fasting in the month of Ramadan; giving money to the needy; and making a pilgrimage to Mecca, known as *hajj*. The men at the Minneapolis-St. Paul airport were fulfilling the ritual prayers.

THE SLAVE TRADE

Followers of Islam have had a long presence in the Americas. Muslim traders accompanied Columbus on his voyage to the West Indies in 1492, and Muslims may have traveled to this continent even earlier. A permanent Islamic presence in America took root during the transatlantic slave trade. Many of the African slaves sold by slave traders to plantations in the American south were Muslims. Kunta Kinte, the ancestor of Alex Haley, who told his story in the book and television series *Roots*, was a Muslim born in Gambia, captured and enslaved in 1767. He had learned the Quran and used to scratch Arabic phrases in the dirt when he was a boy, but the practice of Islam by slaves was forbidden, and they became Christian.

The second wave of Muslim immigrants arrived in the Midwest starting in the 1880s from several countries, including Syria, Lebanon, Palestine, and Jordan. Many were peddlers, who walked miles every day, toting dry goods, such as needles, threads, and lace, to sell to farmwives isolated on the prairie. One of the first American mosques, the Islamic

After the war in Kosovo ended in 1999, hundreds of ethnic Albanian refugees came to the United States in search of a new beginning. Here, some of these refugees participate in a Muslim prayer service at Fort Dix, New Jersey, in May of that year.

house of prayer, was built in Cedar Rapids, Iowa, in 1934. A plain building with a dome and a spire with a crescent on top, the mosque had signs in English and Arabic. Between 1947 and 1960, another influx of Muslim immigrants arrived from Palestine, Yugoslavia, Lebanon, and Egypt. Mosques with minarets rose up in cities and suburbs throughout the United States. Then in 1999, Muslim refugees from the war in Kosovo (in Southern Serbia) began their American journey in a refugee camp in New Jersey.

Thus, today's estimated 5 to 7 million Muslim Americans are not a homogenous group but represent a variety of ethnicities, languages, and traditions. Some are immigrants, while others were born in the United States. Many are converts. About one-third of these immigrants are from Pakistan and other countries in the Indian subcontinent, while one-third are Arab immigrants or converts of other nationalities. The remaining one-third are African American, many of them part of the Nation of Islam. The Nation of Islam was founded in Detroit, Michigan, in 1931 by Wallace Fard Muhammad as a religious and black nationalist group. The Nation of Islam became more prominent under the leadership of Elijah Muhammad during the late 1950s and early 1960s. After Elijah Muhammad's death, his son W. D. Muhammad moved the religion to the more traditional Sunni Islam teachings. Then in the late 1970s, Louis Farrakhan and his supporters split off and revived the Nation of Islam as a black nationalist organization. In 2000, the two groups reconciled and began a period of closer unity.

ISLAMIC IDENTITY

For a long time, Muslims lived outside the American mainstream, overlooked and ignored. Yet they were participants in the country's daily life. By World War II, many Muslim's were serving in the U.S. military. Still the armed services did not recognize Islam. There was no symbol of Islam for Muslim servicemen to wear on their identification tags so that they could receive proper burial rights if they were killed.

A World War II veteran, Abdallah Igram, from Cedar Rapids, Iowa, approached President Dwight D. Eisenhower to ask that the military recognize Islam, just as it recognizes the Protestants, Catholics, and Jews. Igram raised money among Islamic organizations to pay for the dog tags that said "I am a Moslem. There is but one God, and Mohammed is his prophet." "We don't want to convert others, just inform them," said Igram to a reporter at a meeting of Ohio Muslims in 1953.[105]

New immigration laws in the 1960s gave preference to professionals, and many Muslim students, engineers, and doctors were able to emigrate, creating a middle-class Muslim population in the United States. As they became more settled, they had the resources to build mosques and community centers. The Muslim Students Association was founded in 1963 to reach out to Muslims at universities. From 1994 to 2000, the number of mosques in the United States grew by 25 percent, from 962 to 1200, according to a report by the Council on American-Islamic Relations (CAIR), a nonprofit advocacy group. The majority of the mosques were in cities and suburbs, and most of the attendants were male. The worshippers included South Asians, African Americans, and Arabs. Almost all of the mosques used English as a primary language during worship.

For a long time, Muslims in the United States were scattered, looking inward in their local communities, and separated from other Muslims by cultural and ethnic differences. Even before September 11, 2001, a movement began to create a unified Muslim voice in the United States. National Islamic organizations became more visible as they tried to build bridges with outside communities. The Arab American Institute (AAI) was established in 1985 in Washington, D.C., as a nonpartisan organization to encourage Arab Americans to get involved in politics and civic life. Not all of the some 3.5 million Arab Americans are Muslim, but many are. The AAI aimed to create a sense of national identity and community, while still encouraging people to acculturate to American society. Over the years, the AAI has hosted presidents and vice presidents at their conferences. After the events of September 11, the AAI and other Arab and Muslim groups were called on to defend their constituents from being perceived as terrorists. With a sense of trepidation sweeping the country, it was not easy.

The aforementioned Council on American-Islamic Relations tries to promote justice and correct misconceptions about Islam and Muslims. Just days after the September 11 attacks, President George W. Bush met with CAIR leaders at the Islamic Center of Washington, D.C., to talk about easing tensions. Recently, CAIR launched an "Islam in America" advertising campaign to counter anti-Muslim sentiment. One of their advertisements stated: "American Muslims condemn all acts of terrorism and we are as outraged as our fellow Americans by the atrocities committed in the name of God and our religion." Another advertisement shows a photograph of Dr. J. Aisha Simon, a family physician, wife, and mother, who is also involved in international relief work. The words above the photograph state: "I'm an American and I'm a Muslim." Through this and other efforts, CAIR hopes that more people will understand that Muslims are individuals and are not all terrorists.

ISLAMIC SCHOOLS

In part to strengthen their children's Islamic identity, some parents send their children to the growing number of private Islamic schools. Starting in the 1930s, the Nation of Islam has run its own schools, but very few Islamic schools were available for immigrant communities. Beginning in the late 1980s, mosques in cities from New York to Chicago opened their own Islamic schools for local children. An estimated 235 full-time Islamic schools, enrolling about 3 percent of Muslim students, are now operating, according to a 2006 conference on Islamic Education at the Woodrow Wilson International Center for Scholars.

Many Muslim parents choose Islamic schools because they worry that their children do not learn enough about the values and beliefs of their religion. They also are concerned about the attitudes they might pick up in public schools.

The Council on American-Islamic Relations (CAIR) was founded in 1994 to promote Muslim civil liberties in the United States. Here, CAIR members prepare a registration table during the organization's annual conference in 2004 to discuss the role of Muslim voters in that year's presidential election.

Typically, Islamic schools require uniforms, and girls in fourth grade and higher are required to wear a hijab, the Islamic head scarf. Students say afternoon prayers every day, and have classes in Islam and Arabic, along with regular academic classes. "My father's family survived in Bosnian society as a minority for centuries. To survive, you have to know who you are,"[106]said Saffiya Turan, who helped to start Noor al Iman School in South Brunswick, New Jersey. Her father emigrated from Yugoslavia.

A handful of schools go a step further and focus entirely on religion. In a small mosque in Flushing, Queens, New York, young boys ages 7 to 14 spend their school days

A BRIDGE-BUILDER: CAPTAIN HUMAYUN S. M. KHAN

On June 8, 2004, Captain Humayun S. M. Khan, of Bristow, Virginia, was killed trying to stop suicide bombers from attacking an army base in Baquba, Iraq. While standing guard at the gate, Khan, who was 27 years old, saw an orange taxi approaching the base. He feared it might be carrying suicide bombers. He told his soldiers to "hit the dirt," and he stood in front of the moving vehicle to try to prevent it from entering the base, according to the *Washington Post*. The taxi blew up and Khan was killed, along with two Iraqi civilians and two suicide bombers. An additional 10 soldiers and 6 civilians were injured.

Although anti-Muslim sentiment became more prevalent after the September 11, 2001, attacks and during the Iraq War that began in March 2003, Khan is one of thousands of American Muslims who serve in the U.S. military. With about 1.4 million active-duty soldiers in the armed forces, fewer than 4,000 soldiers are declared Muslims. Islamic groups say the number may be as high as 10,000, including many who are African American. Military recruiters are trying to create better relationships with Muslim American communities in order to

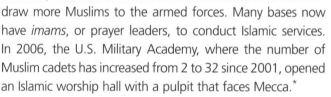

draw more Muslims to the armed forces. Many bases now have *imams*, or prayer leaders, to conduct Islamic services. In 2006, the U.S. Military Academy, where the number of Muslim cadets has increased from 2 to 32 since 2001, opened an Islamic worship hall with a pulpit that faces Mecca.[*]

memorizing the 6,200 verses of the Quran. The students, who are mostly immigrants from Pakistan and India, are participating in a tradition that is still unusual in the United States, but not unusual in Islamic countries. The memorization school is run by the Muslim Center of New York. Students do not study math or science, but only the Quran. When they successfully memorize the Quran, they achieve the highly respected title of *hafiz*. They will be able to participate in the tradition of reciting the entire Quran during the month of Ramadan, the holiest Islamic holiday.

Born in the United Arab Emirates to Pakistani parents, Khan grew up in Silver Springs, Maryland. His parents had fled Pakistan in the 1970s, when it was under military rule, and they sought freedom in the United States. He graduated from John F. Kennedy High School and earned his bachelor's degree from the University of Virginia. Khan joined the ROTC to pay for law school and planned to become a military lawyer. Khan was an outgoing man who loved to play basketball. At his dorm in the University of Virginia, he often served as a peacebroker between white and black basketball players who refused to play with each other.

Stationed in Germany, he was sent to Iraq in February 2004. In Iraq, he started a program to hire Iraqis to work on the base to help improve relations between the U.S. soldiers and the local Iraqi citizens. He also counseled mentally troubled soldiers, according to the *Washington Post*. His soldiers loved him. "They did not call him Captain Khan. They called him 'our captain.'"** said his father Khizr Kahn. Khan was buried in Arlington National Cemetery. He was posthumously awarded a Purple Heart and a Bronze Star.

---

* Richard Whittle, "Uncle Sam Wants US Muslims to Serve," *Christian Science Monitor*, December 27, 2006, 3.

** Stephanie McCrummen, "Looking for Logic Amid the Pain," *Washington Post*, March 22, 2005, B01.

"In this life, kids are doing a lot of things. This is something for God,"[107] one parent, Iftkhar Ahmed told Michael Luo, a reporter for the *New York Times*. His 11-year-old son, Zawar Ahmed, recently became a hafiz at the mosque.

One mother decided to send her son to the school after the terrorist attacks made her more aware of her Islamic identity. Still, while the parents are pleased to see their children's progress, some realize that non-Muslims might be suspicious of the memorization school. One mother, a doctor, who sends her two sons to study there, was reluctant to tell coworkers about the school. "I think they would have a hard time understanding," she said. The students usually take two to three years to memorize the Quran. As for the boys, they told the *New York Times* that they are proud of what they're doing. "I'll be the first hafiz Muslim baseball player," said one of them.[108]

HIJAB OR HOOPS

Briana Canty faced a difficult choice. The Florida sixth grader had to decide whether to play in her team's basketball tournament, or respect her religious customs. In the spring of 2005, Briana was at an Amateur Athletic Union (AAU) tournament in Orlando, where she was to play forward for her AAU team, the Tampa Extremes. Briana wears hijab, a traditional Islamic covering, in this case a scarf, as an expression of her Islamic faith. Tournament officials let Briana play in the first game, but before the second game, they said the scarf violated player rules banning head coverings and jewelry during games. She had to remove the scarf or sit on the bench.

Hijab can be a simple scarf or full body covering. Wearing a veil is a woman's personal decision, but it often becomes a public issue. Reaction to head coverings in the United States has varied. Although the First Amendment guarantees the right to religious expression, this right is balanced against other interests, such as safety in sports and in the workplace, for example. Sometimes, public discomfort with hijab is also an issue. "Hijab is a very visible symbol that one is a Muslim. Unfortunately, they see that and they jump to the next conclusion: 'Muslim terrorist' or 'Muslim fanatic' and it scares them,"[109] said Faiza Ali, director of the New Jersey office of the Council on American-Islamic Relations.

Bans against Muslim women wearing veils in the U.S. Navy, police departments, and even as inmates in jails have made the news in recent years. Some schools have dress codes prohibiting head coverings in order to discourage gang-related dress, but the rule has also been applied to Islamic scarves. In 2003, an 11-year-old girl in Muskogee, Oklahoma, was suspended from her public school for wearing a scarf. Under pressure from civil liberties groups and the U.S. Justice Department, the school later reversed its decision.

Among Muslims, opinions differ on whether—and how completely—women must be veiled. Islamic teachings require that women dress modestly, yet modesty is open for interpretation. In some Islamic countries with secular governments, such as Turkey, women's veils are perceived as more of a political statement than a religious choice, and hijab is discouraged. In Iran, women had to wear veils after Muslim fundamentalists took over the government in 1979. There is also debate about what veiling means to women. Critics say veils restrict women from full participation and equality in society, but advocates say the tradition allows them personal religious expression and pride in their Islamic identity.

Briana refused to remove her scarf and temporarily sat out the game. Meanwhile, her mother called the Florida Council on American-Islamic Relations, which contacted game officials. By halftime, the officials agreed to let Briana play. Briana, who also competes in soccer, track, and volleyball at her middle school, was determined to wear hijab and play sports. "I hope that other Muslim girls do the same thing that I did so they can stand up for their religion because our religion needs to be stronger,"[110] she told the *St. Petersburg Times.*

A MUSLIM GOES TO CONGRESS

Starting in the 1990s, a coalition of American Islamic organizations launched efforts to get more Muslims to the polls and to encourage Muslims to vote as a block. "Muslims for many years have been a bit hesitant, and some of it stems from a good portion of our community coming from parts of the world where voting hasn't been a tradition or even allowed. So it is something that people have to learn when they come to this country,"[111] said Ibrahim Hooper of CAIR. For the 2000 presidential election, CAIR and several other groups, including the American Muslim Council, worked together to get the vote out. They put together voter registration kits and hung voting signs in mosques.

Advocates want to see Muslims get involved in issues that affect them, both here and abroad. In communities with large Muslim populations, their vote can give them a voice in local issues that affect their daily lives. "You pay taxes. And the issue is, should we allow those tax dollars to be used for the purposes of justice, mercy, compassion, which are Islamic values, or should our absence then dictate how that money is going to be spent and be determined by others? To us, political activity is an Islamic responsibility,"[112] said Salam Al-Marayati, executive director of the Muslim Public Affairs Council, which promotes Islamic identity and educates non-Muslims about Islam.

Despite the growing number of Muslims in the United States, only a few have been elected to political office. In 1991, Charles Bilal, an African-American Muslim from Kountze, Texas, became the first Muslim mayor. The number of Muslims in office actually decreased after 2001, according to a report by Al Jazeera, the Arab-language news service. As of 2006, there were three Muslim politicians at the state level—State Delegate Saqib Ali (D-Maryland), State Senator Larry Shaw (D-North Carolina), and State Representative Saghir Tahir (R-New Hampshire). That year, Keith Ellison, a Democrat from Minnesota, became the first Muslim elected to the House of Representatives. The Islamic community welcomed this significant event. "His election tells extremists (both at home and abroad) that America is bigger than they can imagine it to be,"[113] wrote James Zogby, president of the Arab American Institute, in the *New York Daily News*.

Like many African American Muslims, Ellison converted to the religion as an adult. Born in 1963, he was raised in a Roman Catholic family in Michigan, the son of a psychiatrist and a social worker. He became a Muslim when he was a college student at Wayne State University in Detroit. For a short time, he was involved in the Nation of Islam, but Ellison later denounced what he felt was its anti-Semitism.

In November 2006, Keith Ellison became the first Muslim member of Congress when he won the open seat for Minnesota's 5th Congressional District. Ellison is pictured here with his wife, Kim, and Speaker of the House Nancy Pelosi during his swearing-in ceremony on January 4, 2007, at the U.S. Capitol.

Ellison, who is married with four children, became a criminal defense attorney, and an activist in Islamic organizations.

Ellison created a firestorm when he declared that he wanted to be sworn into Congress with a Quran, the Islamic holy book, rather than the traditional Bible. He had learned of a Quran, once owned by Thomas Jefferson, which was in the Library of Congress. Ellison's decision sparked criticism by some, including Representative Virgil Goode, a Republican from Virginia. "I fear that in the next century we will have many more Muslims in the United States if we do not adopt the strict immigration policies that I believe are necessary to preserve the values and beliefs traditional to the United States of America and to prevent our resources from being swamped,"[114] said Goode. Radio talk show host Dennis Prager also attacked the use of the Quran for a swearing-in ceremony on the Townhall.com Web site, saying that using the Quran meant "the Islamization of America" and "undermines American civilization." Many people were happy to see the Quran used for this purpose, and to see a Muslim elected to Congress.

LOOKING TO THE FUTURE

For American Muslim young people, life is full of contrasts. Balancing the modern world and Islamic teachings is not easy for anyone, especially teenagers. Feda Eid, who emigrated with her family from Lebanon to Massachusetts in 1982, watches her favorite shows on television at night after she prays toward Mecca with her family. She wears sneakers and a head scarf. In her spare time, she plays basketball and reads the Quran. During Ramadan, she and several other Muslim students at North Quincy High School near Boston pray in a room at school. Feda was a high school freshman in September 2001. After the attacks, other students began bothering her about her head scarf. "They thought that because I'm a Muslim, I must agree with what the terrorists did. Of course I don't," she told *The Christian Science Monitor*. Feda felt confident and proud of her Islamic identity. "I don't see why anyone would think I'm more or less of an American just because of my religion."[115]

Sometimes teens have difficulty trying to reconcile the values in contemporary American society and the ideals of Islam. While America prizes democracy and individualism, Islam emphasizes community and submission, said Khadeeja Abdullah, a graduate student at the University of California, Los Angeles, speaking to the *Los Angeles Times*. Practicing her religious beliefs sometimes makes her stand out. Strangers on the street have called her a ninja because of her black scarf, which she started wearing after September 11 as an affirmation of her Islamic identity. Abdullah decided that through volunteering in her community, she could better integrate her American and Islamic identities. She knew that community service is one of the Five Pillars of Islam. So along with her academic responsibilities, she volunteers at a health clinic, tutors, and is starting a shelter for the homeless. "I figured out my responsibility within my community and within American society. It is to give voice to the voiceless,"[116] she said.

9

Where Our Roots Start

Nowhere in the country are the issues of identity and diversity more hotly debated than on college campuses. With affirmative action under fire, college admissions officers are looking for new ways to attract diverse student bodies, while protecting academic standards and equal opportunity for all applicants. Many colleges offer special programs to welcome incoming minority students and counseling to help them if any issues arise. When students arrive on campus, they, too, wonder how to balance, or even discover, their own identity within the larger college community. On many campuses, students in racial, ethnic, and other minority groups find each other in clubs, dining halls, and even dormitories.

At Stanford University in Palo Alto, California, students can choose to live in one of four cross-cultural theme houses, each for a different minority group—Chicano/Latino; American Indian, Alaska Native, and Native Hawaiian; Asian American; and black and African American. Students living in these dorms gain support and a sense of cultural identity. The theme houses also reach out to the larger community and host campus events, such as concerts, author readings, and films and lectures. They sponsor celebrations like Cinco de Mayo and Asian Pacific Islander Heritage Month.

Residents do not have to be a member of the ethnic group, but the school gives priority to those who are.

Some people question whether this kind of voluntary segregation hurts the cohesiveness of the student body. In a 2002 report entitled "Racial Paternalism/Separatism in Higher Education," the New York City Civil Rights Coalition, a nonprofit civil rights watchdog group, criticized ethnic houses and other campus programs that promote ethnic identity, saying that colleges are encouraging students to become separated, rather than coming together for greater understanding. "Many of these racially based houses make it very clear in their mission statements that their goal is racial consciousness and identity, thus precluding the concept of a unified campus," the report stated. It went on to say that remedial programs targeted at minority groups unfairly stigmatizes them and lowers expectations. Programs that target only particular groups can lead to stereotyping, miscommunication, and prejudice, the report stated.

"HOUSE OF THE PEOPLE"

Many people disagree, saying that ethnic houses offer support systems and a sense of identity to students, and help them become better students and members of the college community. For American-Indian students at Stanford, a place to call home is often a real help. The Muwekma, the tribe native to the San Francisco Bay area near Stanford, named the dorm "Muwekma-tah-ruk," which means "house of the people," when it opened in 1971. About 30 students live in the house, according to the *Stanford Daily* newspaper. "For natives, coming from small reservations, coming here is a bit of a culture shock. . . . I think if they couldn't relate to other [natives like themselves] their resiliency would be very low,"[117] said Jerry Simmons, one of the student residents. The ethnic-theme dorms also help celebrate students' different identities and cultures. The ethnic-theme dorms "provide a network of support for the community and expose the larger Stanford campus to the culture we celebrate,"[118] said Carmen Gutierrez, a resident assistant at Campus de Casa Zapata for Hispanic students.

THE STRUGGLE ON MAUNA KEA

Whether on a college campus or in the "real world," the balance is always precarious between America as a melting pot, where different groups of people eventually become acculturated and even lose their ethnic identity and traditions, and the nation as a diverse, multicultural "stew," where differences are preserved and celebrated. In the State of Hawaii, where native Hawaiians or other Pacific Islanders make up about 22 percent of the population, people are struggling to find that balance. Since the 1970s, the *Aloha 'Aina* ("love of the land") movement has tried to protect the history, culture, environment, and native language of Hawaii. Many of the island's native Hawaiians have sought to save age-old traditions and values from being lost to both assimilation to American culture and the development of their islands. One of the places where the struggle has been most difficult is on the windy, often snow-capped, summit of a dormant volcano on Hawaii's Big Island.

POLIAHU AND PELE

Rising majestically out of the rain forests, Mauna Kea, reaching 4,205 meters or 13,796 feet above sea level, is the tallest mountain in the Pacific Basin, and one of the most sacred places on earth for native Hawaiians. The "White Mountain," as Mauna Kea means in English, represents a direct connection to the creator. Native Hawaiians used to bury their ancestors on the northern slopes. "In the olden days, when our grandparents, they die . . . then that's

Hawaii's Mauna Kea, or white mountain, is one of the most sacred places on Earth for Native Hawaiians. The W. M. Keck Observatory also stands on top of the mountain, which has made it difficult for Native Hawaiians to worship and bury their dead.

when we take the people where they want to go. Like my grandparents, they came from Kalapana side so they like to be up Mauna Kea mountain facing towards Kalapana. In 1944, we took them up there," recalled local resident Arthur "Aka" Mike'ele Mahi in an interview for the public television documentary *Mauna Kea—Temple Under Siege*. "But people come over here that don't have aloha for our *kupuna* [elders], they don't care. Now the mountain get lot of building. We don't know if the bones have been dug out or the bulldozer push them over the side."[119] According to Hawaiian legend, the snow goddess Poliahu lived on Mauna Kea. She fought with her sister Pele, the goddess of volcanoes, who made Mauna Kea erupt, melting the snow and driving Poliahu away. Finally, Poliahu created a blizzard with snow so deep that Pele fled to her home on Mauna Loa, another volcano on the Big Island, and the fires on Mauna Kea went out forever. Even today, in an ancient Hawaiian tradition, families bury their babies' umbilical cords on the mountain top.

CINDER CONES AND OBSERVATORIES

Because of its importance to Hawaiian culture, another feature of Mauna Kea—which is one of the best spots on earth for astronomers to view the sky—has become a source of conflict. On the broad summit of Mauna Kea, amidst volcanic cinder cones, stands a collection of shiny white and silver domes—scientific observatories with giant telescopes aimed at the sky and manned by astronomers from throughout the globe. With no nearby mountain ranges or city lights to disturb the atmosphere, and the Pacific Ocean stretching for thousands of miles on all sides, this is a prime spot for stargazing. The sky above the volcano is usually clear and calm. The Mauna Kea Observatories, managed by the University of Hawaii, have been the site of many important astronomical discoveries. New moons of Saturn were discovered by Mauna Kea telescopes. In January 2007, scientists at one observatory were studying light emitted 10.5 billion light years away and confirmed the existence of a triple quasar.

Even more telescopes are proposed for Mauna Kea, but in 2006, a district court decided that a better management plan needs to be put in place first. The mountain is also a fragile alpine ecosystem that is a source of water for the Big Island. In determining future development, environmental concerns, as well as the religious and cultural significance of Mauna Kea, need to be taken under consideration. Native Hawaiians serve on an advisory committee to Mauna Kea. After all, Hawaiians hold Mauna Kea close to their hearts, and the astronomers whose life work takes place on its summit also want to take care of it. "That's where our roots start, that's where our island begins, that's where the first rain from Wakea hits, is our mountain," said Pualani Kanahele, a Hawaiian cultural historian and hula expert, in the PBS Mauna Kea documentary. "That's where the first sunlight that rises every morning hits. That mountain is the first for everything we have."[120]

A MULTICULTURAL DEMOCRACY

Like the native Hawaiians who want to protect Mauna Kea, the many identity and ethnic groups throughout the United States live in a diverse and democratic society, where a variety of competing interests tug in different directions. When one group seeks special consideration or a new set of rights, its desires must be weighed against the rights and interests of others. At the same time, sharp differences of opinion often arise. Sometimes these clashing opinions are based on people's fundamental beliefs, so compromise does not come easily. What appears to be just and right to one group may seem wrong and unacceptable to others. Thus, gay marriage, immigration rights, Social Security reform, and other controversial issues that intensely impact particular identity groups can be divisive.

Even so, many clear achievements have been won by the identity and reform groups that emerged in the wake of the civil rights movement. American Indians gained the right to practice their native religion without interference. People who use wheelchairs are able to board a public bus, roll up a ramp to their workplace, and earn a living, even if employers must make adjustments to accommodate their disability. Senior citizens, once left to fend for themselves, are now guaranteed basic medical care, while laws and regulations protect their health and safety in nursing homes. By coming together and pressing for the basic rights that most citizens take for granted, these groups found their voices, as well as a new and lasting pride. No longer on the fringes of society, ignored or rejected, members of these groups were able to become active citizens and contribute their talents to society, thus creating a richer world for everyone.

NO SITTING STILL

There is no sitting still, as rights won one day can be lost the next. Budgets often need to be cut. Programs that were once popular can fall victim to new priorities or political administrations in Washington, D.C., and some battles were never won at all. Despite years of advocacy by civil rights and gay activists, Congress in 2007 had not passed a federal law outlawing discrimination in the workplace based on sexual orientation or gender identity. Employers in 33 states could still legally fire someone based on their sexual orientation, according to the Human Rights Campaign Foundation, an advocacy group. Gay rights groups are supporting a federal law, known as the Employment Non-Discrimination Act, that would protect employees throughout the country in most workplaces, but critics worry this will give preferential treatment to a minority group of employees.

Ethnic and identity groups will continue to grapple with concerns such as this one, sometimes winning, and sometimes waiting longer for the changes they are seeking. Yet the issues will rise to the fore because of the most significant change that has occurred since the 1960s: political inclusion. Many minority groups waited a long time to gain influence in politics, especially on the national level, where they might impact federal laws and policies. They faced obstacles from citizenship to language barriers and voter trust. Despite the challenges, American politics has gradually become more diverse and inclusive. From 1996 to 2000, the numbers of both Asian Americans and Hispanic Americans who cast votes in the presidential elections rose by 20 percent, according to a report by the U.S. Census Bureau. New voices have also entered the political fray. In 2007, Keith Ellison achieved two firsts—the first Muslim American, as well as the first African American from Minnesota to be elected to the U.S. Congress. He brings a vital perspective to national issues at a time when U.S. relations with many Islamic nations are tense. Yet there is a way to go. For most of American history until the 1980s, gay and lesbian politicians could not reveal their identities without risking their careers, and so could not speak out on matters affecting their own lives and communities. Even by the early 2000s, the fear of a backlash against them has kept some gay politicians from

Ben Nighthorse Campbell, who helped sponsor the bill to create the National Museum of the American Indian in 1989, represented Colorado in the U.S. Senate from 1993 to 2005. Campbell is pictured here in traditional Northern Cheyenne clothing immediately after the dedication of the museum in Washington, D.C., on September 21, 2004.

disclosing their sexual orientation, preferring to keep their private lives out of public view.

Still, even a few voices can make a difference. A chief of the Northern Cheyenne nation, Ben Nighthorse Campbell, an outspoken champion of tribal sovereignty, water rights, and other native issues, was the only American Indian on Capitol Hill when he represented Colorado in the House of Representatives from 1987 to 1993 and the Senate from 1993 to 2005. Campbell helped establish the Smithsonian's National Museum of the American Indian. He also brought attention and funding to fight Fetal Alcohol Syndrome, a cause of mental retardation resulting from women drinking during pregnancy, which is a devastating problem on many reservations. Though he was only one legislator, Campbell's presence in Washington, D.C., ensured that the interests of the American Indian would be heard.

Back in April 1963, the Reverend Martin Luther King Jr., sat in jail in Birmingham, Alabama, and considered how crucial it was for every person, regardless of race, ethnicity, or identity, to participate fully in American society. Excluding entire groups of people by giving them fewer rights or unequal treatment, or ignoring them entirely, could only weaken a nation, he believed. "Injustice anywhere is a threat to justice everywhere," he wrote in his famous letter to Alabama ministers. "We are caught in an inescapable network of mutuality, tied in a single garment of destiny. Whatever affects one directly, affects all indirectly. Never again can we afford to live with the narrow, provincial outside agitator idea. Anyone who lives inside the United States can never be considered an outsider anywhere within its bounds."[121] King's beliefs inspired a multitude of ethnic and identity groups then, and in future generations, to step out and step up. With his example, the country would not be the same again.

CHRONOLOGY

1882	Congress passes the Chinese Exclusion Act, prohibiting the entry of Chinese laborers.
1930	Wallace Ford Muhammad starts the Nation of Islam, preaching about black nationalism and Islamic faith.
1935	Social Security Act is passed during the Great Depression, bringing relief to older Americans.
1942	Executive Order 9066 leads to the relocation of Japanese Americans to internment camps during World War II.
1946	In the landmark case, *Mendez v. Westminster*, a California judge rules against the segregation of Chicano children in separate schools.
1947	The National Retired Teachers Association is founded to gain pensions and health benefits; it later evolves into the American Association of Retired Person (AARP).
1953	World War II veteran Abdallah Igram asks President Eisenhower to recognize Islam in the armed services.
1965	The Immigration and Nationality Act, or Hart-Celler Act, opens the door to more immigration from Asia and Africa.
1967	First national table grape boycott is launched by the United Farm Workers of America; the Age Discrimination in Employment Act prohibits discrimination against employees age 40 or older.

1968	Activists found the American Indian Movement (AIM) to promote self-determination and protect treaty rights of Native Americans; Bilingual Education Act provides federal funding for students who are not fluent in English.
1969	Stonewall Riots in Greenwich Village mark the start of the gay rights movement; American Indians occupy Alcatraz Island in San Francisco Bay, demanding that a center for Indians be built on the sacred island.
1970	Senior activists led by Maggie Kuhn found the Gray Panthers to help fight for better services for older Americans.

Timeline

1942
Executive Order 9066 leads to Japanese American internment

1965
Older Americans Act is passed

1968
Bilingual Education Act is passed

1930

1969

1930
The Nation of Islam is founded

1947
The National Retired Teachers Association is founded (later the AARP)

1967
United Farm Workers of America launches national table grape boycott

1969
Stonewall Riots in Greenwich Village draw attention to gay rights movement

1972	Indian Education Act provides new opportunities for American Indian students.
1973	American Psychiatric Association removes homosexuality from its list of psychiatric disorders; American Indian activists take over Wounded Knee, South Dakota, for 71 days; Section 504 of the Rehabilitation Act of 1973 is the first federal legislation to give rights to people with disabilities.
1978	The American Indian Religious Freedom Act protects the practice of native religions.
1981	First cases of a disease later identified as HIV/AIDS are reported among gay men in San Francisco.

1973
American Indian Movement sets in motion standoff at Wounded Knee

1978
American Indian Religious Freedom Act is passed

1990
Americans with Disabilities Act is passed

2006
First Muslim congressman, Keith Ellison, is elected

1970

2006

1970
Maggie Kuhn helps establish the Gray Panthers

1981
First HIV/AIDS cases are reported in San Francisco

2004
Gay marriage is legalized in Massachusetts

1990   President George H. W. Bush signs the
                  Americans with Disabilities Act, the first major
                  civil rights law for people with disabilities;
                  American Muslim Council is organized to
                  increase participation of American Muslims in
                  U.S. politics and public policy.

1993   President Bill Clinton signs the "Don't Ask,
                  Don't Tell, Don't Pursue" policy regarding gays
                  serving in the U.S. military.

1997   The Islamic symbol of a crescent moon and
                  a star is displayed for the first time with a
                  Christmas tree and Jewish menorah at the
                  White House.

2002   The U.S. District Court of Oregon rules that
                  the bones of the 9,000-year-old remains of
                  the Kennewick Man, found in the Columbia
                  River in Washington, be returned to a group of
                  scientists for study.

2004   Massachusetts' Supreme Court allows same-sex
                  marriage.

2007   The first American Muslim Congressman,
                  Keith Ellison (D-Minnesota), takes his oath of
                  office using a Quran.

NOTES

CHAPTER 1

1. Martin Luther King Jr., "Letter from Birmingham Jail." Available online at *http://www.thekingcenter. org/prog/non/Letter.pdf.*

2. Lyndon. B. Johnson, "Annual Message to Congress on the State of the Union, January 8, 1964," Lyndon Bains Johnson Library and Museum. Available online at *http://www.lbjlib.utexas. edu/johnson/archives.hom/ speeches.hom/640108.asp.*

3. Daniel B. Wood, "L.A.'s Darkest Days," *Christian Science Monitor* (April 29, 2002): 1.

4. Cindy Chang, "As American as Vartan, Luis and Na," *New York Times*, October 12, 2006.

5. "Address by César Chávez, President United Farm Workers of America, AFL-CIO The Commonwealth Club of California November 9, 1984—San Francisco." Available online at *http://www.ufw. org/_page.php?menu=resear ch&inc=history/12.html.*

CHAPTER 2

6. Mark Bulliet and Dan Mangan, "Asian Bashing," *New York Post*, August 15, 2006, 25.

7. Thomas J. Lueck, "Two Men Are Accused of a Hate Attack in Queens," *New York Times*, August 14, 2006.

8. Bulliet and Mangan, "Asian Bashing."

9. Jeff Chu and Nadia Mustafa, "Between Two Worlds," *Time*, January 7, 2006.

10. Interview with Maxine Hong Kingston, Leonard Lopate Show, WNYC, September 27, 2006.

11. Frank H. Wu, *Yellow: Race in America Beyond Black and White* (New York: Basic Books, 2002), 80.

12. *United States v. Wong Kim Ark*, 169 U.S. 649 (1898): 731.

13. "San Francisco Clear of All But Six Sick Japs," *San Francisco Chronicle*, May 21, 1942.

14. "An Audience with George Takei." BBC-Norfolk, May 14, 2006. Available online at *http://www.bbc. co.uk/norfolk/content/ articles/2006/04/13/ film_preview_star_trek_ george_takei_feature.shtml.*

15. Timothy P. Fong and Greg Kim-Ju, "Asian and Pacific Islander Americans in

157

Sacramento: A Community Profile, 2000 and Beyond." California State University, Asian American Studies Program, 2001.

16. James Walsh, "The Perils of Success," *Time*, December 2, 1993.

17. Andrew Lam, "Big Politics in Little Saigon," *New America Media*, October 23, 2006. Available online at *http://news. newamericamedia. org/news/view_article. html?article_id=5ea83a995 6aa69770843f4e65f153519.*

18. "Asian Americans Called the New 'Sleeping Giant' in California Politics," UCLA Asian American Studies Center and the UC AAPI (Asian American & Pacific Islander) Policy Initiative. Available online at *http:// www.aasc.ucla.edu/ archives/sleepgiants.htm.*

19. "Sound Barriers: Asian Americans and Language Access in Election 2004," National Asian American Legal Consortium, 2005. Available online at *http:// www.imdiversity.com/ villages/asian/politics_law/ napalc_voting_obstacles_ 0805.asp.*

20. Jun Ilagan, "Filipino American Democrats, Republicans Unite to Increase Clout," *Philippine News*, October 10, 2006. *http://news.ncmonline. com/news/view_article.*

html?article_id=9b5842f233 07da00eb2b5a251e050ba2.

21. Wu, "Yellow," 223.

22. Arar Han and John Hsu, *Asian American X* (Ann Arbor: University of Michigan Press, 2004), 92.

23. Michelle O'Donnell, "Political Trailblazer Is Quick to a Microphone," *New York Times*, August 22, 2006, B1.

24. Ibid.

CHAPTER 3

25. Joseph Shapiro, *No Pity: People with Disabilities Forging a New Civil Rights Movement* (New York: Random House, 1994), 7.

26. Steven A. Holmes, "The Disabled Find a Voice and Make Sure It's Heard," *New York Times*, March 18, 1990.

27. "A Turning Point in American History," American School for the Deaf. Available online at *http://www.asd-1817.org/ history/index.html.*

28. "FDR and Polio—Advocate," Franklin and Eleanor Roosevelt Institute. Available online at *http:// www.feri.org/archives/polio/ advocate.cfm.*

29. "A Look Back at Section 504," National Public Radio, April 28, 2002. Available online at *http://www.npr. org/programs/wesun/ features/2002/504/.*

30. Deborah Kent and Kathryn A. Quinlan, *Extraordinary*

People with Disabilities
(New York: Children's Press,
1996), 177.

31. Susan F. Rasky, "Senate
Adopts Sweeping Measure
to Protect Rights of the
Disabled," *New York Times*,
September 8, 1989.

32. Matthew Van Dusen,
"Desiree Pleads to Use
Special Walker in School,"
Bergen Record, February 20,
2007.

33. Carol Gill, "A Psychological
View of Disability Culture,"
First published in *Disability
Studies Quarterly*, Fall 1995.
Available online at *http://
www.independentliving.org/
docs3/gill1995.html*.

34. Simi Linton, *My Body
Politic: A Memoir* (Ann
Arbor: University of
Michigan Press, 2007), 77.

CHAPTER 4

35. *Mendez v. Westminster*, 64
F. Supp. 544 (1946).

36. Reies López Tijerina, "A
Letter from the Santa Fe
Jail." Available online at
*http://social.chass.ncsu.edu/
slatta/hi216/documents/
TEJERINA.HTM*.

37. Susan Ferris and Ricardo
Sandoval, *The Fight in the
Fields: César Chávez and
the Farmworkers Movement*
(San Diego, Calif.: Harcourt
Brace, 1997), 150.

38. Ibid., 220.

39. Ibid., 267.

40. Interview with Moctesuma
Esparza, "Walkout," HBO.

com. Available online at
*http://www.hbo.com/films/
walkout/interviews/esparza.
html*.

41. Hunter S. Thompson, *Fear
and Loathing in Las Vegas
and Other American Stories*
(New York: The Modern
Library, 1996), 256.

42. Martin Waldron, "Chicanos
Reject 2 Old Parties, Then
Formally Found a 3d One,"
New York Times, September
5, 1972.

43. Judith Baca, *The Art of the
Mural*. American Family,
PBS. Available online
at *http://www.pbs.org/
americanfamily/mural.html*.

44. Sandra Cisneros, *The House
on Mango Street* (New York:
Knopf, 2006), 33.

45. "Rallies Across U.S. Call
for Illegal Immigrants,"
CNN, April 10, 2006.
Available online at *http://
www.cnn.com/2006/
POLITICS/04/10/
immigration/index.html*.

CHAPTER 5

46. Elizabeth Gudrais, "Elders
Demand More Money
for Home-based Care,"
Providence Journal, June 9,
2006.

47. "Letter to President
Roosevelt Regarding Old-
Age Pensions," Social
Security History, Social
Security Online. Available
online at *http://www.
socialsecurity.gov/history/
lettertoFDR.html*.

48. "Presidential Statement Signing the Social Security Act. Aug. 14, 1935." FDR's Statements on Social Security, Social Security Online. Available online at *http://www.ssa.gov/history/fdrstmts.html#signing*.

49. Nell Porter Brown, "Making Things Happen. Political Activism Among Seniors," *Harvard Magazine*, July–August, 2003, 28C.

50. David Cook, "The Point Man on AARP's Controversial Medicaid Move," *Christian Science Monitor*, December 11, 2003.

51. Lawrence Alfred Powell et al., *The Senior Rights Movement: Framing the Policy Debate in America*, Social Movements Past and Present (New York: Twayne, 1996), 118.

52. "President Lyndon B. Johnson's Remarks with President Truman at the Signing in Independence of the Medicare Bill, July 30, 1965," Lyndon Baines Johnson Library and Museum. Available online at *http://www.lbjlib.utexas.edu/johnson/archives.hom/speeches.hom/650730.asp*.

53. Maggie Kuhn, *The Life and Times of Maggie Kuhn* (New York: Ballantine, 1991) 129–130.

54. Eleanor Blau, "Gray Panthers Out to Liberate Aged," *New York Times*, May 21, 1972.

55. "FAA Moves to Correct Injustice of Age 60 Rule," The Seniors Coalition, Senior.org. Available online at *http://www.senior.org/News/Read.aspx?ID=266*.

56. Lincoln Anderson, "With a New Center, Seniors Finally Have the Floor," *Villager*, October 26, 2005.

57. Bill Hogan, "Election 2004: How Older Voters Could Make a Difference," *AARP Bulletin*, October 2004.

58. Jeffrey H. Birnbaum, "AARP Leads with Wallet in Fight over Social Security," *Washington Post*, March 30, 2005, A01.

CHAPTER 6

59. "Stonewall and Beyond. Lesbian and Gay Culture," Columbia University Library Exhibition. Available online at *http://www.columbia.edu/cu/lweb/eresources/exhibitions/sw25/case1.html*.

60. Eric Marcus, *Making Gay History* (New York: HarperCollins, 2002), 28.

61. Ibid., 139.

62. *Lawrence v. Texas*, 539 U.S. 558 (2003).

63. "Supreme Court Strikes Down Texas Sodomy Law," CNN News, November 18, 2003. Available online at *http://www.cnn.com/2003/LAW/06/26/scotus.sodomy/*.

64. "Enough! Enough! Enough!" *Time*, June 20, 1977.

65. Neil Miller, *Out of the Past: Gay and Lesbian History from 1869 to the Present* (New York: Vintage Books, 1995), 409.

66. Claudia Wallis, "AIDS: A Growing Threat," *Time*, August 12, 1985.

67. Ibid.

68. Richard W. Stevenson, "Magic Johnson Ends His Career, Saying He Has AIDS Infection," *New York Times*, November 8, 1991.

69. "Homosexual Sergeant," *Time* (June 9, 1975). Available online at *http://www.time.com/time/magazine/printout/0,8816,913121,00.html*.

70. *Goodrich et al. v. Department of Public Health et al.* Available online at *http://www.masslaw.com/signup/opinion.cfm?page=ma/opin/sup/1017603.htm*.

71. Yvonne Abraham and Michael Paulson, "Wedding Day. First Gays Marry, Many Seek Licenses," *Boston Globe*, May 18, 2004.

72. Ibid.

73. John Cloud, "The Battle Over Gay Marriage," *Time*, February 8, 2004.

74. Ruth Padawar, "N.J. Couple Rings in Law with First Recognized Civil Union," *Bergen Record*, February 19, 2007.

75. Ibid.

76. Marcus, *Making Gay History*, 373.

77. Ibid., 374.

78. Michael Thomas Ford, *Outspoken: Role Models from the Gay and Lesbian Community* (New York: Morrow Junior Books, 1998), 188.

CHAPTER 7

79. Dee Brown, *Bury My Heart at Wounded Knee: An Indian History of the West* (New York: Henry Holt, 1970), 448.

80. Tom Wicker, "Attica and Wounded Knee," *New York Times*, March 8, 1973.

81. Edward M. Kennedy, "Forward," Special Subcommittee on Indian Education, October 30, 1969. Available online at *http://www.tedna.org/pubs/Kennedy/foreward.pdf*.

82. Russell Means, *Indian Activism: Alcatraz Is Not an Island*, PBS. Available online at *http://www.pbs.org/itvs/alcatrazisnotanisland/activism.html*.

83. Richard Margolis, "A Long List of Grievances," *New York Times*, November 12, 1972.

84. Leonard Peltier, *Prison Writings: My Life Is My Sundance* (New York: St. Martin's Press, 1999).

85. Ibid.

86. *Reclaiming Native Land: Alcatraz Is Not an Island.* Available online at *http://www.pbs.org/itvs/*

alcatrazisnotanisland/
nativeland.html.

87. Ben A. Franklin, "Indians'
    Long Walk Winds Up in
    Capital," *New York Times*,
    July 16, 1978.

88. Brodie Farquhar, "Judge:
    Preserve Tribal Religion,"
    Casper Star-Tribune,
    October 17, 2006.

89. Timothy Egan, "An Indian
    Without Reservations," *New
    York Times*, January 18,
    1998.

90. Daniel Kraker, "Edge
    of the Rez: A Stranger
    Among the Hopi," National
    Public Radio, Morning
    Edition, December 26,
    2006. Available online
    at *http://www.npr.org/
    templates/story/story.
    php?storyId=6662251*.

91. "Introduction," National
    Coalition on Sports and
    Racism in Media. Available
    online at *http://www.
    aimovement.org/ncrsm/*.

92. "NCAA Executive
    Committee Issues
    Guidelines for Use
    of Native American
    Mascots at Championship
    Events," National College
    Athletics Association.
    Available online at *http://
    www.ncaasports.com/
    story/8706763*.

93. "NCAI Applauds NCAA
    Decision to Ban Use
    of Indian Mascots in
    Postseason Activities,"
    National Congress of
    American Indians. Available
    online at *http://ncai.*

org/News_View.19+M5
a0b4614bd6.0.html?&
tx_ttnews[arc]=1&tx_
ttnews[backPid]=18&t
x_ttnews[pL]=2678399&tx_
ttnews[pS]=1122
72400&tx_ttnews[tt_
news]=7.

94. Katherine H. Wyrick,
    "Crossing Cultures."
    Bookpage.com, 2003.
    Available online at *http://
    www.bookpage.com/0306bp/
    sherman_alexie.html*.

95. Associated Press, "Reading
    Into Native American
    Writers," CNN, January 10,
    2004. Available online at
    *http://www.cnn.com/2004/
    SHOWBIZ/books/01/10/
    indian.literature.ap/index.
    html*.

96. Susan Logue, "New Lakota
    Leader Puts Emphasis
    on Language," *Voice of
    America*, November 29,
    2005. Available online
    at *http://www.voanews.
    com/english/archive/2005-
    11/2005-11-29-voa42.
    cfm?CFID=102781261&CF
    TOKEN=88499985*. March
    5, 2007.

97. Peter Harriman, "Siege Was
    Wake-up Call for a Culture,
    but Deadly Violence
    Tarnished Movement,"
    Argus Leader, March 16,
    2003.

98. Ibid.

CHAPTER 8

99. Bob Von Sternberg and
    Pamela Miller, "Uproar

Follows Imams' Detention," *Minneapolis Star-Tribune*, November 21, 2006. Available online at *http://www.startribune.com/462/story/826056.html.*

100. "Americans v. Americans," Tolerance.org, The Southern Poverty Law Center. Available online at *http://www.tolerance.org/news/article_tol.jsp?id=275*

101. Ibid.

102. Steve Inskeep, "Between Faith and Country: Muslims in America," National Public Radio, September 11, 2006. Available online at *http://www.npr.org/templates/story/story.php?storyId=6041929.*

103. Eric Gorski, "Identity Search: To be Muslim in America," *Denver Post*, February 11, 2007.

104. Jeff Chu, "Duty, Honor and Allah," *Time*, August 23, 2005.

105. "American Moslems," *Time*, July 13, 1953.

106. Susan Sachs, "Muslim Schools in U.S. a Voice for Indentity," *New York Times*, November 10, 1998. Available online at http://www.jannah.org/articles/nytimesart.html

107. Michael Luo, "Memorizing the Way to Heaven, Verse by Verse," *New York Times*, August 16, 2006. Available online at *http://www.nytimes.com/2006/08/16/nyregion/16koran.html?ex=1313380800&en=bfd66b91d*

e7a7870&ei=5088&partner=rssnyt&emc=rss.

108. Ibid.

109. Associated Press, "Muslims Find Range of Acceptance for Hijab," October 27, 2003. Available online at *http://www.firstamendmentcenter.org/analysis.aspx?id=12120.*

110. Sherri Day, "Muslim Head Scarf Debated," *St. Petersburg Times*, April 5, 2005.

111. "The American Muslim Vote," *Religion and Ethnics Newsweekly*, PBS online, October 20, 2000. Available online at *http://www.pbs.org/wnet/religionandethics/week408/cover.html.*

112. Ibid.

113. James Zogby, "Celebrate Ellisons Oath on the Quran as an All-American Moment," *New York Daily News*, January 4, 2007.

114. Rachell Swarns, "Congressman Criticizes Election of Muslim, *New York Times*, December 21, 2006.

115. Sara Steindorf, "An American, a Muslim, a Teen," *The Christian Science Monitor*, November 6, 2001, 18.

116. Diane Winston, "6 Million Muslim Stories Waiting to Be Told," *Los Angeles Times*, November 20, 2005.

CHAPTER 9

117. Madhavi Devashar, "Campus Defends Its Ethnic Theme

Houses," *Stanford Daily*, November 19, 2002.

118. Ibid.

119. "Burials on Mauna Kea." *Mauna Kea—From Mountain to Sea.* Available online at *http://mauna-a-wakea.info/maunakea/F4_burials.html*

120. "Cultural Landscape." *Mauna Kea—Mountain*

Under Siege. Available online at *http://www.mauna-a-wakea.info/maunakea/F3_culturalland.html*.

121. Martin Luther King Jr., "Letter from Birmingham Jail." Available online at *http://www.thekingcenter.org/prog/non/Letter.pdf*.

BIBLIOGRAPHY

Ferris, Susan, and Ricardo Sandoval. *The Fight in the Fields: César Chávez and the Farmworkers Movement*. San Diego, Calif.: Harcourt Brace, 1997.

Ford, Michael Thomas. *Outspoken: Role Models from the Gay and Lesbian Community*. New York: Morrow Junior Books, 1998.

Kent, Deborah, and Kathryn A. Quinlan. *Extraordinary People With Disabilities*. New York: Children's Press, 1996.

Novas, Himilce, and Lan Cao. *Everything You Need to Know About Asian American History*. New York: Plume, 2004.

Miller, Neil. *Out of the Past: Gay and Lesbian History from 1869 to the Present*. New York: Vintage Books, 1995.

Powell, Lawrence Alfred, John B. Williamson, and Kenneth J. Branco. *The Senior Rights Movement: Framing the Policy Debate in America*. Social Movements Past and Present. New York: Twayne, 1996.

Rosales, F. Arturo. *Chicano! The History of the Mexican American Civil Rights Movement*. Houston: Arte Publico Press, 1996.

Smith, Paul Chaat, and Robert Allen Warrior. *Like a Hurricane: The Indian Movement from Alcatraz to Wounded Knee*. New York: The New Press, 1996.

Wu, Frank H. *Yellow: Race in America Beyond Black and White*. New York: Basic Books, 2002.

WEB SITES

The Arab American Institute
http://www.aaiusa.org/

AARP: The Power to Make It Better
www.aarp.org

Voting and Registration in the Election of November 2004
http://www.census.gov/prod/2006pubs/p20-556.pdf

Gray Panthers: Age and Youth in Action
http://www.graypanthers.org/

Mauna Kea: Hawaii's Tallest Volcano
http://hvo.wr.usgs.gov/volcanoes/maunakea/

MALDEF: Mexican American Legal Defense Fund
http://www.maldef.org/index.cfm

Voting Is Power: Muslim American Society
http://www.masvip.org/index.htm

NCAA Executive Committee Issues Guidelines for Use of Native American Mascots at Championship Events
http://www.ncaasports.com/story/8706763

National Indian Youth Council History
http://www.niyc-alb.org/history.htm

"Politics," Pew Hispanic Center
http://pewhispanic.org/topics/index.php?TopicID=64

Reies López Tijerina: Chicano Protest, 1969
http://social.chass.ncsu.edu/slatta/hi216/documents/ TEJERINA.HTM

The Great Wall Resource Portal
http://www.sparcmurals.org:16080/sparcone/index. php?option=com_content&task=view&id=20&Itemid=52

Social Security Online
http://www.ssa.gov/

UFW: The Official Page of the United Farm Workers
http://www.ufw.org/

Conference on Islamic Education in North America
http://www.wilsoncenter.org/index.cfm?fuseaction=events. event_summary&event_id=172467

FURTHER READING

Cheatham, Kae. *Dennis Banks: Native American Activist.* Springfield, N.J.: Enslow, 1997.

Ferris, Susan, and Ricardo Sandoval. *The Fight in the Fields: César Chávez and the Farmworkers Movement.* Edited by Diana Hembree. New York: Harcourt Brace, 1997.

Han, Arar, and John Hsu, eds. *Asian American X: An Intersection of Twenty-First Century Asian American Voices.* Ann Arbor, Mich.: University of Michigan Press, 2004.

Hockenberry, John. *Moving Violations: War Zones, Wheelchairs, and Declarations of Independence.* New York: Hyperion, 1996.

Red Shirt, Delphine. *Bead on an Anthill: A Lakota Childhood.* Lincoln: University of Nebraska Press, 1999.

Santiago, Esmerelda. *When I Was Puerto Rican.* New York: Vintage Books, 1994.

Shapiro, Joseph. *No Pity: People with Disabilities Forging a New Civil Rights Movement.* New York: Random House, 1994.

WEB SITES

National Coalition on Sports and Racism in Media
http://www.aimovement.org/ncrsm/

The Disability Rights Movement
http://americanhistory.si.edu/disabilityrights/welcome.html.

Gay, Lesbian, and Straight Education Network
http://www.glsen.org

Mauna Kea Observatories
http://www.ifa.hawaii.edu/mko/

The Matthew Shepard Foundation
http://www.matthewsplace.com/

Muslims in America
http://www.muslimsinamerica.org

National Citizens' Coalition for Nursing Home Reform
http://www.nccnhr.org/default.cfm

Alcatraz Is Not an Island
http://www.pbs.org/itvs/alcatrazisnotanisland/

Tolerance.org
http://www.tolerance.org

United Farm Workers of America
http://www.ufw.org/

PICTURE CREDITS

INDEX

ABOUT THE CONTRIBUTORS

Author **ANN MALASPINA** has written nonfiction books for young people for many years. Her books cover many topics, including jaguars, tsunamis, children's rights, and globalization. Malaspina began her career as a reporter for a community newspaper in Boston, Massachusetts, where she wrote about immigrant issues, tenant rights, and poverty. Those stories sparked her interest in people on the margins of society and their battle for recognition and equal rights. She has a bachelor of arts from Kenyon College and a master of science in journalism from Boston University. She lives with her husband and two teenage sons in northern New Jersey, where she enjoys hiking, photography, and travel.

Series editor **TIM McNEESE** is associate professor of history at York College in York, Nebraska, where he is in his fifteenth year of college instruction. Professor McNeese earned an associate of arts degree from York College, a bachelor of arts in history and political science from Harding University, and a master of arts in history from Missouri State University. A prolific author of books for elementary, middle and high school, and college readers, McNeese has published more than 90 books and educational materials during the past 20 years, on everything from Picasso to landmark Supreme Court decisions. His writing has earned him a citation in the library reference work *Contemporary Authors*. In 2006, he appeared on the History Channel program *Risk Takers/History Makers: John Wesley Powell and the Grand Canyon.*